Hannah Moloney is a TV presenter on ABC's *Gardening Australia*, permaculture practitioner, bestselling author and climate activist. When she has a quiet moment, you'll find her in Nipaluna/Hobart gardening, playing the ukulele (badly but happily), trail running (badly but happily), painting birds and hanging with her delightful family.

Why We Garden

On the joy and wonder
of growing things, even
when we don't have to

HANNAH MOLONEY

affirm
press

First published in Australia in 2026 by Affirm Press, a Simon
& Schuster (Australia) Pty Limited company
Wurundjeri Woiwurrung Country
Level 3, 162 Collins Street, Melbourne VIC 3000

Affirm Press is located on the unceded land of the Wurundjeri Woiwurrung peoples
of the Kulin Nation. Affirm Press pays respect to their Elders past and present.

New York Amsterdam/Antwerp London Toronto Sydney/Melbourne New Delhi
Visit our website at www.simonandschuster.com.au

AFFIRM PRESS and design are trademarks of Affirm Press Pty Ltd,
Inc., used under licence by Simon & Schuster, LLC.

10 9 8 7 6 5 4 3 2 1

A catalogue record for this
book is available from the
National Library of Australia

9781923135345 (hardback)
9781761822483 (ebook)

Cover illustrations and interior design by Hazel Lam
Interior illustrations by Hannah Moloney
Line drawings via Shutterstock, Freepik & iStock
Typeset by Post Pre-press Group in 12/16 pt Bembo Std
Printed and bound in China by C&C Offset Printing Co. Ltd

MIX
Paper | Supporting
responsible forestry
FSC® C008047

For my dad

Written on Muwinina Country, Lutruwita/Tasmania
Always was, always will be

Contents

Introduction

If you look at a map of the world, you'll see that I live pretty much at the bottom on a little island called Lutruwita/Tasmania. You'll find me and my family in a bright pink house on a patch of land that's around 3000 square metres with a 30-degree slope that borders Nipaluna/Hobart. Behind us is native bushland that squirms with wallabies, pademelons and an array of birds, while in front of us looms the city and ocean. We look out over Nipaluna/Hobart, the timtumili minanya/River Derwent, the distant mountains and the ever-dynamic sky.

For more than a decade my sweet husband, Anton, and I have lovingly shaped this steep slope into productive terraces. We've filled them with fruit and nut trees, vegetables, cheeky milking goats, chaotic chickens, shy ducks, herbaceous shrubs, native plants, a stunning greenhouse, flurries of flowers, a unicorn sculpture, our sassy daughter, Frida Maria, and Olly, our dog who's also known as Little Bro or Sacred Angel. It's all love.

We pour ourselves into this landscape and in 'real-estate speak' have over-capitalised. But we don't care about resale value; we care about soil health and soul health. For us, the two are inextricably linked.

But sitting quietly beside the complete adoration we have for our garden is the persistent pulse of how much work we must do to maintain or evolve it. There are regular moments when that pulse spills over into overwhelm and I ask myself … do we really need this amount of garden in our lives? Why grow tomatoes when we can buy them? Why tend flowers that only bloom for a short period before they die and have to be replanted?

Thankfully it's not long before the voice in my head snaps back: 'Oh, shut up, Hannah, just get on with it,' and I go back to gardening.

I do wonder, though, what is it that has made this such an essential part of my daily life?

One of my earliest memories is more of a feeling than a vision. I'm sitting on the grass in our urban backyard. I'm old enough to walk, but not effortlessly. My dad's somewhere nearby because I can hear him working in the garden – the shuffling of his boots and the distant thumping of garden pots being moved around. The sun is soaking my bare legs and the grass is gently prickling the skin between my toes. It feels good and right. I feel good and right.

I was born into a gardening life. A few months before I entered the world, the youngest of five, my family moved into a rambling Queenslander on a quarter block in inner city Meanjin/Brisbane in Kurilpa/West End. I loved (and still love) that house and dream of it often. All open windows, big verandas full of plants and people, creaking timber floorboards, walls heaving with art, photographs and floor to ceiling bookshelves, and wide-open doors welcoming you in. It was the early 1980s and Kurilpa/West End was multicultural magic with Aboriginal and Torres Strait Islander mob, the Anglo-Irish, Lebanese, Vietnamese, Greeks and more mixed in together. There was the strong and delightful presence of poor artists and students and lots of young working-class families like mine, who were flush with imagination and a strong work ethic but not so much cash.

Dad got busy transforming the backyard into what became a thriving herb nursery, which kept him busy for the next two decades. Every spare crack of our childhood was filled with helping Dad in the nursery – which was honestly pretty boring as far as I was concerned. Hot and boring. If I heard Dad coming in one side of the house, I'd hop to and rush out the other side, avoiding him and his inevitable demands for help. I wanted to be roaming the streets with my mates and yarning in gutters, not potting up herbs for my dad.

But my whole adult life has circled around gardening both personally and professionally. In recent years I've come to recognise that there's a type of spirituality wrapped up in it as well. Gardening has been a part of who I am for so long that I rarely stop to ask why. It's just what I do. Like breathing, I don't stop to ask why, I just breathe. But unlike breathing, gardening isn't always an essential task in our modern world. And yet so many of us shape our lives to include moments of hands in earth and bodies bent over baby plants, willing them to live. We spend hours crawling around on our hands and knees pulling weeds, planting trees, tucking in plants with blankets of mulch while talking to them. We're obsessed.

So, why *do* people garden?

As I grow older my curiosity is also growing about the choices people make with gardening. What inspires them to start, and what makes them continue?

To answer this question, I knew I couldn't rely on my sample size of one. So I began to ask around. One day, I was in the small town of Deloraine in northern Lutruwita/Tasmania, giving talks on gardening at an annual craft fair. There I met fellow gardeners, and I asked them what they loved about gardening. One woman said, 'There's just *something* about gardening … *Something* that just keeps me coming back and keeps me there.' Those listening all nodded knowingly. We knew what that *something* felt like – unique to all of us of course – but something we could all relate to.

I kept asking. I talked to my gardening mates and acquaintances. Then I looked further and spoke to well-known Australians. I yarned with authors, a journalist, a landscape architect, Aboriginal and Torres Strait Islander peoples, a former politician and a musician.

But of course, I couldn't just speak with well-known people about gardening! I needed to hear from the everyday gardeners out there, the thousands of Australians who pour their hearts into their patches of earth. So, I conducted a survey. In the end, I surveyed almost 1500 people for this book – an overwhelming amount of garden delight to wade through. The survey results were enlightening. Joy, beauty, money, resilience – there are so many interesting reasons why people garden. This is why I wrote this book. I wanted to dig deep and unearth (so many puns!) the 'why' behind gardening.

Which of the following benefits explains WHY you garden?
Tick as many boxes as you like

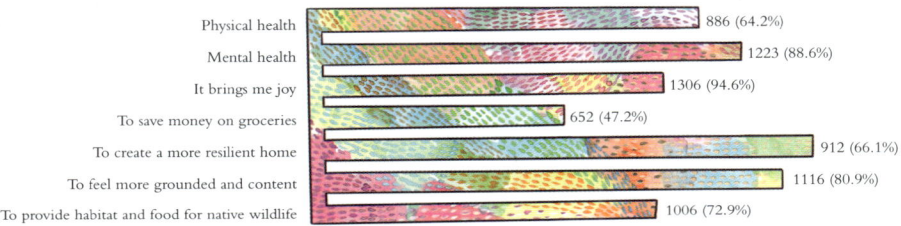

Physical health — 886 (64.2%)
Mental health — 1223 (88.6%)
It brings me joy — 1306 (94.6%)
To save money on groceries — 652 (47.2%)
To create a more resilient home — 912 (66.1%)
To feel more grounded and content — 1116 (80.9%)
To provide habitat and food for native wildlife — 1006 (72.9%)

The private survey I did online

But there's another, more personal reason why I wrote this book. As well as trying to understand the *something* the woman in Deloraine was referring to, I want to understand my own special *something*.

After tending to the soil that I've lived and gardened on for over ten years, I recently had a moment of clarity. I realised that while I'm out there regularly feeding it, nourishing it – all to make it as healthy as possible – the soil is doing the same for me. The soil feeds me, nourishes me and makes me as healthy as possible. The garden is gardening me. It's only healthy when I'm healthy and I'm only healthy when it's healthy.

I know I'm not alone in this deep feeling of connection to plants, and to the earth. It touches on some essential part of being human and alive. When we die our bodies return to the earth. Whether we're buried in the ground, burned, or undergo a sky burial where vultures eat our remains on top of a mountain (as is tradition in parts of Tibet), our bodies change form. They become the earthworm, the ash, the vulture, the bird poo and then eventually, one way or another, they find their way into the soil. The ground beneath our feet is made up of our ancestors. In time, we all become one big, interconnected garden.

Gardening is one of the few activities in modern life that reconnects us to nature in both a practical and invisible way. It's a tangible thread that ties us all – living and dead, human, animal and plant – together into one giant ecosystem. But there's an invisible pulse to it that pulls at my heartstrings. There's a type of spirituality in that interconnectedness. I bow down to it and it holds me up.

Maybe this is my *something*. The juicy feeling of big connectivity that helps remind me that we are the soil, the carrot crop, the compost, the goat manure, the gum tree, the dahlia flowers. The same force of life running through me is also running through my almond trees. We have this in common. Same, same – not different. We. Are. The. Garden.

And if there's one thing we need more of in this world, it's finding what we have in common and focusing on that rather than on what keeps us apart.

This is the miraculous wormhole that this book will spiral down. So, are you ready? Let's get digging.

For survival

Dirty hands,
hard work
Sowing,
harvesting,
repeat
Bowing down
to land

If I wanted to, I could pop down to the shops and come home with bags full of food. I could buy mangoes and watermelon in the depths of a cool temperate Tasmanian winter, thanks to corporate food systems that play God and Goddess with the seasons, and I can source apricots from Turkey and kiwi fruits from China. But it's only a recent phenomenon that we have shops with such a wide variety of food to choose from. For most of human existence, survival involved being actively engaged with where our food came from. Everyone was required to take part in growing, sourcing or processing food in some way. Food production ebbed and flowed with the climate and the land. In some parts of the world, such as in the Global South, this is still the case. But in the wealthier countries that make up the Global North, growing your own food is largely optional. And yet, even in these more prosperous countries, you'll find millions of us spending months pampering patches of potatoes or obsessing over fruit trees when we could just pop out to the local shops and buy produce easily and, generally, affordably. You could comfortably go your whole life without stepping foot into an edible garden. But it wasn't always this way …

Ancient gardeners

You could argue that gardening is written into us. It's part of our animal instinct to survive. After all, the beginning of gardening is considered a major turning point in our history as a species, an instinct that allowed us to thrive and dominate the planet.

Early humans relied completely on what they could hunt or forage from the land; but at certain stages around the world, some of us decided to cultivate the land. We began to plant seeds, to domesticate animals, to control our landscape by clearing trees or lighting fires. These activities gave us a more reliable source of food, and it allowed our populations to grow. With these more sedentary settlements developing we started to see wildly significant evolution in how humans lived. This included economic frameworks such as tax being introduced, changes in our gut microbiomes (as our diets changed) and, in some regions, monotheism. We also started to see the development of widespread social stratification. In contrast to a hunter-gatherer food system, gardening and farming led to having surplus food that could be stored, which meant a number of new roles had to be established. It became critical to divide society into roles that supported this new way of life. According to the World Economic Forum, 'The roles of an administrator, a servant, a priest, and a soldier were invented. The soldier was especially important because agriculture was so unsustainable compared to hunting and gathering.'[1] Because of the ever-changing nature of agriculture, people were migrating into neighbouring regions in search of abundant natural resources, and the soldiers protected their natural assets. Slavery boomed, as farming is hard work and free labour was desired. When you look at it from this angle, gardening and farming has a bit to answer for.

Gardening, which is defined as small in scale and for domestic use only, is thought to have morphed into farming, which is larger, more streamlined and on a commercial scale.

Dominant history puts the first signs of farming and gardening around 11,700 years ago with the beginnings of the Holocene epoch after the last major ice age, when the climate warmed enough to let humans thrive. Around this time, we saw agriculture take off in the 'Fertile Crescent', a tract of land that runs through the Middle East and is often referred to as one of the 'cradles of civilization'. It includes parts of present-day Syria, Egypt, Lebanon, Israel, Jordan, Turkey, Iran, Iraq, Palestine and Cyprus. The area owes its fertility to the abundant water sources from the Tigris, Euphrates and Nile rivers which regularly flooded the region, building up fertile soils.[2] This meant the style of agriculture was sedentary, allowing humans to develop permanent towns and cities around these food basins which supported population growth and helped shape society as we know it.

By 8000 BCE we started to see staple crops such as barley and wheat spread into parts of the Indo/European regions (most of Europe, parts of south-west Asia, the Indian subcontinent and the Iranian plateau), along with the integration of some livestock. It's incredible to think of this practice gradually spreading across the globe, but one of the amazing parts of human history is that different forms of agriculture developed independently in different cultures — cultures that had no contact with one another.

For instance, farming developed in the Americas around 9000–8000 BCE without any interaction with the Fertile Crescent.[3] And in Papua New Guinea (PNG), people living at the Kuk site, in the Wahgi Valley of the PNG highlands, were practising agriculture at least 7000 years ago and possibly up to 10,000 years ago. In fact, there's building evidence that sugar cane and bananas – two of the world's most valuable crops, originated from here.[4][5] Meanwhile, in China and east Asia, staple crops such as rice, millet and soybeans were independently cultivated from at least 7000 BCE. [6]

Australia has its own interesting story when it comes to ancient agriculture. In 2014, Australian author Bruce Pascoe, who identifies as Yuin Bunurong and Palawa/Tasmanian Aboriginal, wrote *Dark Emu, Black Seeds: Agriculture or Accident?* It outlined how Aboriginal and Torres Strait Islander Peoples didn't technically fit the nomadic hunter–gatherer box they had previously been categorised into. Pascoe explains that as he read the early journals from white settlers in Australia he noticed 'repeated references to people building dams and wells, planting, irrigating and harvesting seed, preserving the surplus and storing it in houses, sheds or secure vessels, creating elaborate cemeteries and manipulating the landscape – none of which fitted the definition of hunter-gatherer'.[7]

As Pascoe helped articulate, Aboriginal and Torres Strait Islanders managed the country strategically with in-depth planning and what's referred to as 'fire-stick farming'. Also known as cultural or cool burning, fire-stick farming is a land management technique that helps look after the health of vegetation, Country and culture. In contrast to a blazing bushfire, fire-stick farming is controlled, low and slow with the fire 'walking' across the land strategically. With this approach, Aboriginal Australians farmed and managed the land, creating a 'mosaic of trees and grasslands that meant the highly combustible Eucalyptus forests were not likely to create intense bushfires'. This approach to producing food differs wildly to agriculture in the Fertile Crescent because their landscape, rainfall and fertility differs widely.

Recent evidence suggests that the practice of fire-stick farming is at least 11,000 years old and could go back as far as 40,000 years.[8] This method of farming allowed Indigenous Australians to grow grain (which they then made into flour to bake bread), foster perennial root crops, and manage wildlife movements and feeding grounds for efficient and seasonal hunting. But they didn't do it in fenced-off paddocks or in a capitalist framework of individual ownership and gain.[7]

Tim Flannery elaborates: 'As the term firestick farming suggests, the Aboriginal use of fire resembled agriculture in some ways; it yielded certain crops at certain times, suppressed weeds and was carefully controlled.'[7]

Aboriginal author and scholar Tyson Yunkaporta explains that, despite natural disruptions, such as volcanic activity, Aboriginal people managed to maintain stable situations in landscapes for thousands of years:

We stabilise these landscapes and climates and then we hold them as long as we can, but ironically that means we have to be moving around on it seasonally. So we're not sitting in permanent sedentary communities and built environments. But we were establishing a permanence in the stability of our climate and bioregion.[10]

But it's not just environmental management that creates stability – it's social management too. In his refreshingly no-frills style, Yunkaporta goes on to say:

But that's only as good as your neighbours. Make sure you marry your neighbours, and you adopt your kids across – it's the only way from stopping them from fucking everything up. Cause the guy up the creek from you – if he's shitting in the water then your kids are going to get sick.[9]

Working with the land and strategically intervening in Nature to ensure stability is clearly a central part of how many cultures survived and thrived, just as it was in the Fertile Crescent and Mesoamerica. The practices are dramatically different, but then again so are the soil types, water access, population and land area. The Fertile Crescent was based along a river system, on incredibly fertile soil. In contrast, Aboriginal and Torres Strait Islander farming practices were conducted across massive tracts of land that relied on rain for irrigation and featured some of the oldest soils in the world without deep layers of fertile topsoil. The type of agriculture prasticed in the Fertile Crescent isn't a natural fit for the Australian landscape. It's like trying to put a square peg in a round hole by transferring a type of agriculture that relies of deep, fertile topsoil and abundant water into a place that is severely limited in those things. Unfortunately, since European colonisation this has become the dominant type of agriculture, to the detriment of the Australian landscape.

Our thin layers of topsoil are compromised with routine tilling and excessive quick-fix fertilisers that lead to long-term problems. Meanwhile our rivers and underground water aquifers are put under enormous pressure to grow often water-hungry crops. Our dominant approach to agriculture in Australia is based on degradation instead of regeneration.

In contrast, Aboriginal Australia responded to the land and climate to create a type of agriculture that made sense. They moved across the country strategically to manage the health of their available resources, ensuring they weren't plundering and degrading their land, but regenerating it constantly.

For many of us, this Fertile Crescent style farming is all that we know, and we find it hard to imagine another way of gardening. We also find it hard to separate our own gardening from the Western economy that our lives and agriculture are now built around. The economics of Indigenous Australian agriculture wasn't based on how much cash was in the bank, but on how healthy the ecosystem was and how well relationships were built and maintained across clans.

This is not a natural mindset for many of us. We may not *need* to garden to survive, to ensure a healthy ecosystem or to build social ties, but some of us might feel the need to grow a garden to be secure.

Money

For many people, money equals security. One of the reasons I embraced edible gardening as a young adult fresh out of home was to save money. As a student and activist, my tiny budget would've died of shock at any organic produce shop. It was the edible gardens I helped create and tend to in all the share houses I lived in (twenty-five over ten years!) that kept me in abundant greens and veggies. Australian author Tim Winton was the same: 'When I was young and broke, with kids to feed, the kitchen garden was sometimes the difference between barely surviving and living well.'

While establishing a garden can be done on the cheap, it can also cost all the spare dollars you have. I've built gardens with nothing except the existing soil and donated seeds. I've built large gardens in rental homes for around $100 where I salvaged most materials from the side of the road and through gardening networks and then paid for some compost and plants. And then there is my current garden.

At the time of writing, Anton, Frida and I are twelve years into living and gardening on this patch of Muwinina Country. Despite being just under one acre, this patch has a cheeky habit of swallowing up any spare cash I might have on things such as fencing, a greenhouse, mulch, compost, plants, earthworks, boulders, goats, garden tools and more plants. But these days (post the major establishment phase) most of these additions are optional. Instead of spending money on travelling, clothes shopping, horse riding, mountain bike riding or any other money-hungry hobbies, I like to spend it on materials for Anton to build us a bespoke greenhouse (it looks like something out of a fairy tale). This is how my family and I choose to spend money. Luckily for me and Anton we're equally obsessed and excited about things growing – we're both soil and soul mates.

I guess it really depends on how you look at it. One time, Anton was helping our landscaping friend on a garden job, building a large wildlife-proof enclosure for food production. The clients spent a whopping $20,000 on the job – all to grow some fruit and vegetables. Why? Because they're doing it to secure good food, activate their landscape and create a thriving home. It's their values coming into life. Priceless.

But there are many, many people who create gardens with not much and who quickly save money on buying food. I've included a tiny sample of the hundreds of responses I got when I asked this question to my online community.

- 'I grow mizuna, endive, radicchio, leek and silverbeet, and I reckon through each winter I've saved $150 on veg over three months that supplements things that are cheaper like carrots and onion.' **Lauren**

- 'I started gardening to have access to healthier food that I couldn't afford to buy at the time. Of course it has evolved into so much more now. I once actually weighed and calculated the dollar value of everything I grew for six months. It averaged out at around $60 a week over six months.' **Jordy**

- 'I resigned from my teaching job to be a full-time artist and expanded my garden beds especially so I could feed myself. I'm very much a "learning as I go gardener". I made relishes, froze what I could and it's going well. I am a poor, but not starving, artist!' **Georgia**

- 'I do exclusively organic gardening and when I compare organic produce prices, especially on perennials like some of my herbs, raspberries and strawberries, I think I'm saving close to US$200 each season alone … I haven't purchased raspberries, frozen or fresh, in at least two years … We are also certainly saving money on plants that have decided to become self-seeding like cilantro (haven't bought seeds for that in years), daikon radish, and Napa cabbage.' **Sophia P**

- 'Growing all my own fresh herbs and salad greens is definitely a money saver for me. Bagged salad and herbs wrapped in plastic are so expensive ($3+, a bunch of herbs and a packet of seed is cheaper) … and they're easy to grow from seed. High yielders like pick-and-come-again silverbeet/kale, green beans, snow peas, zucchini and pumpkins also save me money on groceries.' **Erica Monique**

- 'We grow almost all our own fruit and veg and produce

our own eggs. We started for fun, kept going for sheer enjoyment – rather than for savings. But now, it definitely does save us money … and it gives us a much more diverse diet than we'd otherwise have. I doubt I'd ever have eaten cape gooseberries, tomatillos, or spent July gorging on kiwi fruit and passionfruit if I wasn't ploughing through a glut of them from my own garden.' **Melissa Pollard**

- 'I definitely grow to save money but also for health plus the joy of growing and eating my own produce. I rarely spend more than $10 a week for vegetables plus my eggs are pretty much free as I sell my excess quail and duck eggs for feed money.' **Lindy Saler**
- 'I hate gardening but I do it to get home-grown organic food pretty much for free.' **Anonymous**

Food security in times of disruption

Done well (moderately well even), gardening can save you some cash, which is an ever-increasing necessity for people in a world where the cost of living is rising. But beyond the benefits to your hip pocket, there are also benefits to your sense of security.

When I interviewed Tim Winton, something he said to me really hit a nerve: 'I think [gardening is] an old instinct, the body memory of being broke and anxious. When there's nothing in the fridge and nothing in the bank, there'll always be food in the garden. So it's probably a security thing. Like knowing you have a couple of tanks of rainwater.' For me, it's the feeling of knowing that I can take care of myself regardless of what the world throws at me – which seems to be an increasing number of disruptions (hello global pandemic, climate crisis and natural disasters). All around the world, individuals, communities and large entities are getting organised for disruptions.

When I think of gardening and security, I think of the Svalbard Global Seed Vault on the Norwegian island of Spitsbergen in the remote Arctic Svalbard archipelago. Established in 2008, it houses tens of thousands of seeds to protect the world's food supply from natural disasters, conflict, disease, the climate crisis, pests or sabotage.

Another example of this type of seed saving initiative is the Vavilov Seed Collection in Leningrad, Russia. Named after the geneticist, plant breeder and biologist Nikolai Vavilov, it was established in 1921 and housed over 370,000 seeds from around the world. It 'became one of the greatest contributors to crop diversity conservation and use in history'.[8] Vavilov's primary goal was to end world hunger by creating a secure and reliable food source by selecting and breeding the most robust varieties possible. His motivation came from his childhood where he witnessed mass starvation in his country when an early and harsh winter wiped out crops.

Despite all his work, he was arrested in 1940 by Stalin's secret police on charges of spying for Britain. While he was in jail, World War II tore through Europe and Leningrad came under siege by German forces. They cut the city off for 890 days from 1941 to 1944 leading to the deaths of 800,000 people from starvation. Vavilov himself died of starvation in 1943 after spending two years in jail. Included in the deaths are a group of botanists who barricaded themselves inside the Vavilov Seed Collection and starved to death while guarding its 370,000 seeds from German soldiers.[9] They valued the seed collection more than their lives; they recognised its importance in establishing future food security. Good, robust and viable seed is the foundation to any healthy food system.

To this day, the Vavilov Seed Collection remains the world's largest (and oldest) collection of plant genetics with 'meticulously cataloged seeds hailing from all over the earth'.[10] These scientists were saving seed (and gardening) for the good of the world. Their 'why' for doing so was based on securing not just *quality* of life, but simply life itself.

In today's modern world, as temperatures rise and arable land is degraded, there are increasing threats to both our quality of life and life itself. Tim Winton doesn't bother beating around the bush with his view:

> When you try to grow food in challenging environments, you have a much more visceral understanding of fluctuations and trends in climate … Our culture's dependence on, and captivity to, burning fossil fuels is making our environment hotter and often drier. It's also making the human world less and less just. For a gardener north of Capricorn and south of Cancer, it's getting harder to grow things in the open. Yields are lower, growth periods are shorter and more intense. Adverse events are more extreme. On current trends, climate extremes will get steadily (or quickly) worse. When you grow things, this is not an abstract concept. In recent years I've had to contend with the idea of people in parts of Australia having to resort to taking kitchen gardens inside altogether. Not a charming prospect.

In among the survey responses I received was one that had a tone as equally fierce as Tim's. It was from a woman named Linda Woodrow: 'My conscious reasons [for gardening] are political. I've always thought that the phrase "permaculture is a revolution disguised as organic gardening" felt true, and in the context of climate change, even more so. But also, there is probably a subconscious motive lurking in there [for me] … knowing I can always feed myself and my loved ones makes me feel safe.'

Tim and Linda's sentiments about gardening resonate deeply with me. During the Covid-19 pandemic, when supermarkets were stripped bare and the global supply chain glitched, I absolutely felt safe. We had our large and pumping edible garden. We had abundance.

When we're told by climate scientists to expect more disruptions, it's not a hysterical idea to have a food garden, it's a darn sensible one.

Dr Norman Swan says that:

Our food supply is at risk of drought, floods, fires, temperature change, landslides, sea level rise and ocean warming. Sea rises will cause massive human migration and the potential for even more environmental disruption and exposure to new micro-organisms. Extreme heat will kill people and limit the ability of outdoor workers to do their jobs. If the natural cycles of water, carbon, phosphorus, and nitrogen collapse, so will the future of many on our planet because agriculture will collapse as well.[11]

Dr Gretta Pecl AM, a professor in marine ecology at the University of Tasmania and one of the world's leading climate scientists, has stated something similar: 'I think we are headed for major societal disruption within the next five years … [Authorities] will be overwhelmed by extreme event after extreme event, food production will be disrupted. I could not feel greater despair over the future.'[12]

When I read this quote from Dr Pecl I too was filled with

despair. She happens to live in Nipaluna/Hobart and we've crossed paths a few times, so I decided to reach out. It turns out there's more to that quote. When we caught up, Dr Pecl told me that while she did say that, to her disappointment, the journalist left out the second part of the quote which was that despite this despair she chooses active hope and throws her energy behind that. Because at the end it's more useful to get active, not anxious. Active hope means being an active participant in shaping the future we want rather than passively witnessing the opposite.

In our own small ways, it seems that many of us who garden share this 'why' and the urge to get active. Of the 1380 people I surveyed, 912 of them said that they garden 'to create a more resilient home and community in the face of climate change'.

We're joining the dots; we know that there can be no thriving future if we don't act now. Our gardens, paddocks and urban green spaces are the perfect place to start.

Sanctuary thinking: A survival mindset

Choosing action over anxiety is one of my favourite 'sanctuary thoughts'. When I'm finding the politics of the world too hard to stomach, have read too many climate science reports and am feeling a bit scared and sad, I slide into 'sanctuary thinking'. What does this mean? Well, basically it means that I research, learn from and mull over practical ideas full of active hope that inspire me to keep going. Human beings are an incredibly resilient bunch and we have an impressive track record of getting active and doing useful things to help the common good.

Cuba in the 1990s is the perfect example. After the Soviet Union collapsed, all resource support (food, fossil fuels and more) to Cuba ceased almost overnight and the country entered a severe economic crisis that became known as the Special Period. This was coupled with embargoes from America, meaning they were effectively cut off from the world. They experienced major disruption. Cuban people got really hungry really quickly. But then they got organised and established a world-renowned urban agriculture system where they skilled up to feed themselves. Their main city of Havana, home to 2 million people at the time, was transformed into a series of urban farms with livestock integrated throughout. Was it easy? Of course not. Did many people suffer? Absolutely. But overall was a localised, abundant and organic food system established? Yes.

In recent years, the Food and Agriculture Organization of the United Nations has documented that around 400,000 thousand workers now work in urban agriculture across Cuba. Using only organic methods, urban farms have provided 70 per cent or more of all fresh vegetables consumed in some major cities across the country.[13] And in late 2024, the Urban, Suburban and Family Agriculture Program recorded more than 1.3 million tons of fresh vegetables harvested in Havana, an increase of 36,000 tons from 2023.[14] These days Cuba has diversified its offerings (away from only exporting sugar) and has re-engaged in some global trade,[15] meaning it now imports some food and resources. However, it still prioritises local agriculture and maximises landscapes in the name of food security and food sovereignty.

The example of Cuba illustrates my sanctuary thought: if we need to, if climate change disruptions demand it of us, we can establish urban food production in our towns and cities.

My sanctuary thought includes knowing that myself and

others have skills in growing food, organising community, project management, making compost, keeping livestock, building rain tanks and compost toilets, preserving food, and more. And sure, does this make me sound like a paranoid prepper? Maybe a little. But these are age-old skills that stem from common sense that just isn't so common anymore. I think of them as incredibly useful 'forever skills'.

I want to emphasise that sanctuary thinking isn't about escaping. It is the exact opposite. It's about dissecting real-world examples of people finding motivation, strategies and techniques to act meaningfully and effectively to survive and thrive – despite the politics of the times. And, when you seek them out, there are hundreds of wonderful examples of people choosing to act. Interestingly, so many of them start in the garden.

More and more, people are growing food in response to their concerns about climate change's impacts on our food system. It's definitely one of the key reasons I embraced gardening as a young person. By eighteen, I had learned about the big challenges of the world (mainly climate change) and thought, 'How can I be most *useful* in this world, for this world?' Within a few years of exploration, I landed on two things; working with people and place. In particular diving into helping to grow community and grow food! This was how I chose to be useful in the world. It aligned with my natural interests, not to mention my childhood growing up around gardening, and so I went for it … in a major way.

And, according to my survey, I'm not alone in seeing gardening not only as an act of security, but an act of climate activism.

- 'It gives me a small sense of peace and control in a world of anthropogenic climate change, industrialisation, waste, expense etc. Enables me to feed my family healthy food on low income.' **Anonymous**

- 'I do it because I want to teach my children how to be self-sufficient and remember the past.' **Sarah T**
- 'Gardening allows me to make a small difference in a changing world. Improving the soil and habitat in my garden helps me feel positive about the future.' **Anonymous**

For joy

They planted
a seed
It erupted,
face to sun
They planted
ten more

My home office and writing desk looks out over our garden. Dahlia heads bop happily in the breeze, fruit trees stand strong showing off their edible jewels, goats bleat, chickens cluck, and the greenhouse that my sweetheart, Anton, built from scratch is a work of functional art. It's a pitched roof structure made from recycled hardwood, old windows and red bricks. It even includes a small stained-glass window his maternal grandmother, Dorothy, made many decades ago. On good weather days I can push open my massive office window and feel like I'm sitting in the garden while doing my work. I can hear the bees buzzing, see birds diving through the air and feel a gentle breeze on my skin. And just beyond my garden is a view of Nipaluna/Hobart and the timtumili minanya/River Derwent running into the ocean. The whole scene could be from a fairytale. Each time I glance up I'm hit with a type of shocked joy and gratitude that I get to live here. It's a feeling that travels from my heart and whooshes up my throat before settling into a smile in my eyes. It's just so bloody beautiful that I can hardly believe it.

Joy is different to happiness. Happiness is a fleeting guest that visits for a short moment, like when my husband brings me a steaming cup of ginger and black tea in bed in the morning. But joy is a long-term resident, a slow-release contentment. Like the connection my husband and I have – strong, stable and laced with kindness and a shared delight we have in one another.

Gardening is fertile ground for joy to grow from. When you harvest those sweet potatoes, smell that flower or crunch into a fresh carrot, satisfaction and contentment rushes from your fingers to your mouth and nose, fluttering through your heart on the way.

My first garden of my very own was a rusted-out wheelbarrow planted with pansies that I created with Dad when I was seven. It involved my dad doing most of the work and me ever so carefully planting seedlings, tucking them in firmly, but not too firmly, just like Dad showed me. I was very proud. But I have to admit that my pride didn't really translate to diligent gardening. I'm pretty sure Dad mostly kept the plants alive. But as I rushed past the barrow on my way to one of my treehouses, cumulative delight washed through me every time and settled in my bones. And when the annual flowers came to their natural end, I impatiently waited/demanded for the next lot of flowers to move in.

Growing up, my siblings and I had two treehouses: one in our backyard in the macadamia tree and the other in our neighbour's garden – he let us build one in his mango tree. In the true style of 1980s/1990s parenting, we were largely unsupervised kids. We'd push the trampoline beneath the macadamia tree and jump out of the treehouse onto the fenceless trampoline and try to stop our bodies from whirling off into the nearby garden beds. Amazingly no bones were broken. We'd spend hours doing this, cracking macadamia nuts in between bouts of jumping to sustain our fearless playing.

And then there was the mango treehouse. It was built across two old mango trees planted close to one another. We'd walk back and forth on our badly built bridge (again, its amazing no bones were broken) and pig out on mangoes. Bare feet, hot subtropical air on my skin and sticky mango juice running down my chin, my shirt and my arms. When it comes to living a good life, I was really living it and didn't even know it.

I think it's basic human nature to only want to do things that make us feel good. As a kid it felt really good to clamber through the landscape, which was our gardens. After all, cityscapes are still landscapes.

Gardening is scientifically proven to make us feel good. Australia's Commonwealth Scientific and Industrial Research Organisation (CSIRO) states that coming into contact with soil can release our 'happy hormone': specifically it's contact with a soil bacteria called *Mycobacterium vaccae* that triggers the release of serotonin in our brains.[16] This is why some folks refer to gardening as a natural antidepressant.[17]

So when you find yourself out there in the garden wondering how you got there and maybe even why you're there, the reason is likely to be simply that it makes you feel good: that it brings you joy.

In my online survey, the most popular multiple-choice option for why people garden was 'it brings me joy', with 94.6 per cent of people giving joy a big fat tick. Joy was also a recurring theme in a lot of my interviews.

[Gardening] is a wonderful thing. I was recently in a logged area and I took off the edge of the road a little native pepper (*Tasmannia lanceolata*) and brought it home in my handkerchief because it was going to be destroyed by the next round of logging … and I've got it in a little tube in the garden at home now, and just seeing it lift its head up and then start to grow is just a beautiful feeling – life unfolding, and that's always (whatever the species is) a joy to experience.

These are the words of environmentalist and former Greens leader and environmentalist Bob Brown. I have such a visceral image of Bob kneeling on the edge of a clearfell and gently folding his hanky around a baby native mountain pepper plant. Bob's over eighty years old now, not a spring chicken, and there's something so moving about the image of an elderly man kneeling to pick up young life.

And Bob is absolutely correct! Witnessing life unfolding is pure joy. It's nothing short of magic. Bringing plants back from the brink of death never gets old.

One year, Anton bought me an indoor plant, which was risky business at the time as growing plants inside wasn't a strength of mine (it still isn't, if I'm honest). Despite really loving it and trying to keep it alive, I almost killed it. When things 'fail' in my garden I have an unhelpful habit of going into a bubble of denial. This can look like many things, but in this case it involved putting the pot plant outside near my shed and not looking at it for months – like, *many* months. Until one day I looked at it and realised there was a tiny green shoot at its base: it wasn't completely dead! I gave it a harsh prune, repotted it with fresh mix into a larger pot and watered it. And guess what happened? The bloody thing grew back and it's currently looking quite wonderful.

The amount of joy that flooded through me from resurrecting that indoor plant was unreasonable, but I let it flow through me anyway. That tiny green fleck of life kicked my butt into gear – I had to meet this new life halfway to help it thrive. And just so you know, at the time of writing I haven't killed an indoor plant for at least one year – we can all learn new skills when we choose to.

My type of joy

When I think of what type of joy gardening has gifted me, there's an underlying, constant foundation of joy that holds me up and sometimes even holds me together. But there are also specific memories that rise to the surface. Here are just a few.

The joy of cheeky friendship: When Anton and I got married, our wedding was like a three-day festival with around 150 friends and family all staying on a property in country Victoria. It was a very DIY affair where people bought food to share, we brewed the beer, we sewed napkins and screen-printed love hearts on them all, Anton made my wedding dress, my bouquet was a bunch of parsley – you get the idea. Our gorgeous friends and family delighted us with their company and showered us in love and some beautifully special presents as well. One memorable present was from our friend Danny: it was a massive stash of seeds from the Diggers Club, one of Australia's best nurseries. On each packet Danny had written hilarious, romantic, ridiculous, sexy and fun comments related to that particular vegetable. I cannot tell you how much joy we got from that present for months and years to come. Every season I'd go into our seed stash, find what I needed, spend five minutes laughing out loud and then the rest of the gardening session giggling to myself over whatever inappropriate comment Danny had written.

The joy of knowing you can grow food anywhere: When I lived in a converted horse stable in inner city Naarm/Melbourne with Anton, there was no actual earth in the tiny courtyard available to us. When I say courtyard, it was just a concrete footpath down the side of another house. We promptly built a raised garden for our herbs and salad plants. It was a mix of relief and joy to remember that we can grow food anywhere, even when there's a thick layer of concrete between us and the Earth.

The joy of building soil: Living in so many rental properties, I embraced no-dig gardening, which is a quick way of building soil for edible gardening (developed by Australian gardener Esther Dean in the 1970s). I smothered some lawn with damp cardboard, layered old straw with horse manure, green garden waste and more straw, and watered it thoroughly. I planted immediately into pockets of compost and watched as the cucumbers of my dreams grew. I built fertile soil and felt like a queen as a result.

The joy of organising for change: I spent five years working with four friends to turn around half an acre of compacted weedy lawn into what became Hobart City Farm. For those years the team fed hundreds of households and built soil health, and the farm served as a living demonstration of what urban food systems can look like. It's since been transformed into the David Stephen Neighbourhood Garden and Nipaluna Nursery, growing native plants. But the legacy of collaboration and gardening joy lives on. It's a constant reminder that cityscapes are still landscapes and that our food system can be shaped by us – that's you and me.

The joy of surprise and delight: Every year I forget that my daughter and I planted some tulip bulbs under a number of fruit trees and every year I get completely surprised in late winter and early spring when they pop their bloody beautiful heads up and say hi. I was talking with a local farmer Jilly Middleton one day and she referred to flowers as 'joy on a stick'. It's the best description I've ever heard.

The joy of pattern language: Everywhere I go across this beautiful country I see all types of gardens and meet all types of gardeners. Without exception there is a shared language that runs between us all. It's a pattern language of being able to read soil types and plant species, and understand how water moves through a space. And then there's the relationship between the gardener and the garden. Sure, I might not know everything about them and what they're up to, but we can all sense the relationship in progress between them and see it in motion. I love that shared language – it's an instant connector.

The joy of beating the blackbirds: One year the local population of the non-native blackbirds spiked enormously (after a solid rainy period). For the next three years our orchards underwent a lot of pressure from them as they'd try to pick off the young fruit or nuts when they were small and green, before I had time to net them. So the joy of getting in before them and netting our cherry trees before they knocked them off was immense. Then later in the season there was the joy of harvesting bulging bowls of plump red cherries and feeling like I'd won! It reminds me of a golden bit of advice from fellow *Gardening Australia* TV presenter Sophie Thomson about pests and diseases in the garden. She said that instead of reaching for the fungicide/pesticide/chemical fix, sometimes you just have to wait pests and diseases out for a season or two and things will self-regulate in the garden ecosystem. After those few years of blackbird pressure, there was a hotter and drier than usual season and it eased off as their population decreased. Things come and go.

The joy of Muwinina Country: Muwinina Country includes Nipaluna/Hobart and surrounds and is where we've been able to own land for the first time ever (along with the bank). The feeling that washed over me on securing our home and land was unexpected. I thought I was feeling fine. But when we were able to buy this place, I felt safe, grounded, deeply grateful, and a rush of joy at being able to put down my roots – literally. At the time of writing, we've lived here for almost twelve years and not a day goes by when I don't look around and pinch myself that I get to live here. Multiple times a week I'll loudly declare that 'I love living here' and my daughter responds in an annoyed voice with 'Yeah, yeah we know, Mama.'

The joy of Frida Maria: Apart from her much-loved ducks, these days my daughter isn't overly interested in the garden. But she still has an unusual amount of information on gardening and livestock in her brain for a ten-year-old. She can sow seeds, plant crops, assess when things need harvesting, identify countless crops and milk goats. Am I disappointed that she currently doesn't want to spend all her time in the garden? Not at all. Because I know it's all in her – she has a stack of practical skills available at her fingertips. She also knows the effort involved in gardening with all the cultivating, processing and tending required. Frida also understands where our food comes from and has an appreciation for it. Sometimes she'll declare, 'Other kids at school don't have gardens like ours, Mama, can you believe it!?' Or: 'We can never ever ever leave this house and garden. This is our forever home and I will live here forever.' Her pretend indifference but fierce connection makes me giggle and delivers washes of joy into my heart. No matter what she does with her life, she's got the garden as a foundation for everything else to grow from.

The joy of growing a giant, useless pumpkin: When Frida Maria was a tiny baby I participated in a local 'how big a pumpkin can you grow' competition. My competitive spirit was like, 'Fucken oath! I wanna win!' I sourced some seeds from a type of pumpkin known to grow massive and to taste like wet cardboard. Perfect. With sleep deprivation and a baby under my arm I pampered this useless pumpkin so it would grow as big as possible. Unfortunately, at some point I think sleep deprivation won out. The pumpkin was still a hefty guy – well over 60 kilograms – and dwarfed my baby, but it would have benefited from more regular feeding. Sadly, I didn't win, but there's nothing like some healthy competition to get some joyful adrenaline flushing through your veins. Many laughs were had over the sassy banter between gardeners across the growing season, and the delight in growing something big and useless was surprisingly delightful for a functional gardener like me. When the season ended, the pumpkin was too heavy to move so I just left it in place and gradually cut it into chunks to feed to my compost systems.

Joy personified

I've never met someone who oozes joy as much as Costa Georgiadis. As the leading host of ABC TV's *Gardening Australia* he is constantly on the road, talking, singing, educating and inspiring all ages to get out into the garden and connect with Nature.

Somewhere there's a photo of when we first met. Now, Costa is a shorty who fits perfectly into the nook of my armpit. But me? I'm

6 foot 2. In this photo of our first meeting, he's crouching down to exaggerate his shortness next to my tallness. We're both laughing. It was around 2008 in rural Lutruwita/Tasmania at a small community gardening gathering. I knew who he was from his SBS TV show *Costa's Garden Odyssey,* but meeting this hairy fuzz ball of joy was like a combination of being hit with pure sunshine and a semitrailer. We became friends, and I'm beyond stoked to work alongside him now on *Gardening Australia* (my dream gig). The amazing thing about Costa is that when he's with you, he's *really* with you – nothing and no one else matters. He treats everyone the same, whether you're a six-year-old school kid, politician, movie star, grassroots activist, farmer or nanna. It's like he gives us all permission to shine.

When I asked him why we bother gardening he replied:

Why would you garden?' Why *wouldn't* you garden!? It's the simplest way to connect to the earth! People had a very prescriptive and limited perspective of gardening for a long time. And it was this idea of something that your grandparents or your parents did, or what you aspire to do when you retire … And I was like, why would you wait that long?! Why would you put it off?

For people like Costa and me, gardening is like breathing. He can't imagine his life without it.

I've watched Costa in action with crowds of adults and kids for years now and without fail he injects instant hits of happiness into pretty much everyone who comes in his orbit. His joy of gardening is infectious. I reckon that these bursts of joy also sow seeds of joy in people's heads and hearts. These seeds continue to grow and take root, helping people to connect with Nature and find their own special type of joy.

- 'As I work in the garden, the garden works on me! Whether it's my veggie garden, the native garden for bees and birds or the fruit trees, it all gives me such joy, connection to place and wonder.' **Anonymous**
- 'Mainly because it brings me so much joy [and] grounds me through my cancer diagnosis [and] treatment.' **Tamara Taylor**
- 'Connection with the physical world in a way that makes you again feel the joy and wonder of childhood. Nature, gardening, the cycle that is both complex but simple – it's magic. Best thing for my mental health by a long way.' **Lisa Watts**
- 'I garden because it brings me such joy. I generally feel the garden calling to me. I go out every morning to check in with it. I just can't imagine not being able to garden.' **Therese Denman**
- 'For the joy of admiring a plant as it matures and flowers, the joy of something I grew being on my dinner plate. I could sum it up when I pick a perfect fresh fig off my tree and eat it on the spot, in the sun.' **Anonymous**
- 'It makes me feel good when I garden, it makes me feel good to share it with others, and it makes me feel good when we have worked hard in the garden and you get to see the rewards. It's wonderful.' **Simone B**

Because it's beautiful

Soil
between toes
The hum
of gardens
growing
Buzzing in
my bones

Beauty is everywhere once you let yourself see it. It's in the spring blossoms, the freshly weeded vegetable garden, the wild bushland noisy with birds, the out-of-control orchard, the pile of compost, the sharply pruned hedges and the decomposing mulch wriggling with microscopic life.

But it's also in the gardener. In their hands as they reach down to work the soil; in their stiff, creaking backs as they spread yet another load of compost around the fruit trees; in their hopeful minds as they sow new seeds for new life.

Despite this, you'll find there are different interpretations of what makes a garden beautiful – often laced in judgement and an informal, sometimes subconscious, hierarchy of which type of garden is superior, depending on culture and context.

For example, if there was to be a battle between ornamental and edible gardens I would historically be on the side of the edibles. Once upon a time I would snub the ornamental garden as a waste of space (sorry). It just seemed pointless to spend energy on growing plants that I couldn't eat. But in recent years, I'm happy to say I've learned that pretty much all gardens are galaxies of blissful beauty no matter what form they take.

For thousands of years, humans have seen our gardens as an ultimate symbol of beauty. The word 'paradise' is derived from the Persian word *pairidaezas*, meaning 'walled garden'. The notion of paradise as a garden predates Islam, Judaism, Christianity and even the Garden of Eden. It stems from the Sumerian period 4000 BCE in Mesopotamia.[18]

In harsh environments, these walled gardens provided sheltered microclimates for plants to thrive. While always aesthetically formal, these walled gardens originally included fruit trees. However, over the centuries, they evolved to be purely ornamental.

Some of the people I surveyed online singled in on beauty as part of their reasons for gardening.

- 'Food gardening is an act of love for my family. My ornamental gardening provides food for my soul.' **Alicia Cooper**
- 'Feeds my soul, love the creativity and surprise.' **Anonymous**
- 'To bring more beauty and joy to the world.' **Anonymous**
- 'Plants are beautiful; nature is incredible. And it feels beautiful and incredible to be a part of it.' **Steph Roughley**
- To create a beautiful ever-changing space I'm proud of and love to be in. It brings me joy to know I created it.' **Anonymous**

- 'I look out the window, and there are so many shades of green that I can't count them all. I love to see the increasing number of insects, worms, birds, lizards and other creatures that now make their home alongside us.' **Becky**
- 'Creating a beautiful space, nurturing that space, then sharing that space with all the creatures who visit or live in it, gives me joy.' **Gaynor**
- 'It allows my artistic side to bloom and watching all the critters come to visit my patch is utterly magical.' **Kylie Watkins**

Around an hour out of Sydney, where Mickey Robertson has created a picture-perfect expansive garden at her property, Glenmore House. It's the type of garden you'll find in fancy books and magazines and where people come to have special events. A work of art, grounded in the love and talent of Mickey's design eye – it's a genuine beauty. While not as formal as French garden design it still uses hedges and clean lines to create garden rooms that slowly morph into surrounding paddocks and bushland. Close to the house the garden is more formal with courtyards, feature trees, hedges and roses. It then morphs into large vegetable gardens, orchards, trees, mixed perennials and a field of flowers before giving way to paddocks and native bushland.

I spent a couple of days in this garden filming with ABC TV's *Gardening Australia Junior*. And when I wasn't in front of the camera I took myself on little treasure hunts, peeking over or around hedgerows to find the next garden surprise. I found soft pink poppies blowing me kisses beneath fruit trees and stone walls artfully restored. It's a place that left me in quiet awe – with a touch of anxiety knowing how much work goes into creating such a wonderland.

What I really admire is Mickey's eye for design, which any gardener can see when walking into her property. The attention to detail is everywhere. As an interior designer, she sees the garden as an extension of her house and home – she has connected them both seamlessly. Because, as she says, 'We can't be in the garden all the time, but I view the garden literally as an extension of the detail of each room in the house. And looking in *from* out should be just as expected as from inside *to* out, so plants are placed to suit.'

When Mickey and her partner Larry first moved there, they made 'a lot of mistakes'.

> [I was] under the misapprehension that in 'moving to the country' it was all about green pastures ... and early notions of cottage gardens filled with foxgloves and delphiniums soon had to be given up for where we really are ... in a more Sydney-esque climate, so the early years were filled with learning and experimentation.

And maybe this is why I was still thinking about Mickey's garden months after visiting: the plant selection is obviously strategic, suiting both the soils and the climate. It's dripping with health, something which I increasingly believe is a key ingredient for a beautiful garden. It looks like it belongs – not imposing itself on the land, instead it's of the land.

I picked up this thread of thought again after seeing photos and videos of nurserywoman and gardener Lou McLachlan's property. She and her wife, Deb Clarke, have gardened up a storm in Mollongghip, Victoria. What used to be a flat paddock is now a stunning ornamental garden with a large collection of formal hedges creating different garden rooms. Generous gravel paths guide people through the spaces flanked with mass plantings, trees and more hedges – all with stunning sculptures and artworks placed strategically for maximum impact.

Lou describes her style of gardening as semi-formal; she likes the boundaries you can create with plants. Hedges can form clear lines which grow into garden rooms which Lou can play in front of and in with different plants.

She puts her attraction to this style of gardening down to her personality.

There is an element of control. I do like controlling the environment. I'm putting together what I want other gardeners to see. A bit like a recipe – there needs to be some order; if you don't do it right then you can ruin the whole recipe. All the plants have to enhance one another. I go over and over the garden design – I drive my wife crazy – as every season I change or tweak things. The main intention is that everything offsets and complements each other.'

Walking through her ornamental garden, Lou describes it as if you're walking through a plant album. Everywhere you look is another perfectly framed photo for you to enjoy: 'Each room is a chance to do something different. I look at each section like a photograph and ask myself what I want it to look like.

When I ask her what makes a beautiful garden, she says that 'beauty is something you need to feel as well as see'. The strongest feedback she's had from opening up her gardens for people to walk through is that people are blown away by how healthy things are.

Regardless of gardening experience, 'people can recognise a healthy garden and it really makes them feel something.' She goes on to say that calmness and order also make a garden beautiful for her. 'I know you can get this in a wild park, but when you're presenting a garden there's got to be balance with colour and form'. Undoubtedly, this careful curation creates beautiful gardens that can leave people relaxed and calm, but it seems that a *healthy* garden is the non-negotiable foundation on which this has to be based.

While Mickey's and Lou's meticulously designed gardens are different to my predominantly edible sprawling garden, we have quite a few things in common. A focus on soil and plant health is the most obvious, but there's also a lot of love flowing through our patches: it's oozing out of the tree bark, the carefully crafted structures and juicy-leafed vegetables from pumping kitchen gardens. The three gardens are the products of many years work, many sighs of overwhelm and many sparks of delight. And there's deep beauty in that. We've all created our very own versions of paradise that speak to us and the land on which we live.

Whose idea of beauty?

Anton and I open up our garden to the public a couple of times each year. A few weeks before opening we spend many hours weeding, pruning, mulching and 'beautifying'. Hundreds of them come through each time and it's always fun and interesting to talk with people and hear their thoughts and questions. On one of these days, a well-meaning man summarised his thoughts on our patch: 'Yeah, it's a pretty chaotic garden, with some order here and there ...' Ouch! And here I was thinking it was looking neat and tidy. Beauty is subjective, of course, and ultimately when it comes to aesthetics, it's only yourself you need to please. So, I love my garden, chaos and all.

But it did get me thinking. What makes a garden beautiful for other people?

In pursuit of this question, I went along to an open garden day around Nipaluna/Hobart for ornamental gardens. One garden stood out to me. It had a box hedge maze, rose garden, fountain, and an unusual ornamental espaliered fence line that started around 1.8 metres high. It reminded me of French garden design, which 'is a very formal, very ordered gardening style with lots of straight lines and symmetry'.[19] I have also heard French garden design described as a type of design that imposes order onto Nature. I stood there for a while noticing how the garden made me feel and how other people were reacting. I realised that this garden sounded different to my own garden. In the stunning garden of hedges and roses I could close my eyes and hear the quiet and the twinkling of the small fountain. In my own garden it's comparatively noisy with a cacophony of humming, buzzing, tweeting, chortling and croaking of life, similar to when you're out bush camping or walking.

It was undeniably beautiful – the shades of green on green, the clean lines, the tinkling of the fountain – but I realised that my shoulders had turned into tight little knots.

I think it's the amount of work involved in maintaining such a manicured piece of garden art that makes me twitch. Even when standing in Mickey's beautiful garden, a vibration of tiredness crept through me at the thought of the maintenance required. Does a beautiful garden need to be relaxing? No. But for me there's relaxation to be found in beauty, or at least my version of a beautiful garden. Chaotic to some, beautiful to others.

I got talking with another visitor called Tina about this. Tina's retired and spends her time walking in the bush painting landscapes and, when it rains, vases of flowers inside. I asked her whether the garden made her feel relaxed. She said no, and when I asked why, she said: 'If you look at the maze, there's only one type of plant and the lines are so crisp. Almost too crisp. But when you turn and look at some of the more informal and diverse flower gardens [in the same garden], your eyes relax and you can feel your eyes moving differently across the colours and forms.'

I did as she said and she was right. Instead of being fixed and static on the box maze, the diverse flower patch had my eyes gliding across shapes and colours and my brain started to melt a little – in a good way: it was relaxing.

Across the globe, one of the most desired elements in a garden for it to be considered beautiful is a lush, well-trimmed lawn. I have a small lawn – although being chemical free, never irrigated and 50 per cent white clover (*Trifolium repens*) it's not overly lush or well-trimmed. But it's a great gathering space for our campfire, to practise handstands and for our little dog to run through. Over the years, I've spent a lot of time encouraging people to downsize or remove their traditional lawns so they can integrate other plants into their garden. Why? Because lawn culture has its runner roots firmly wrapped around the gardening world and can compromise overall ecosystem health in our gardens and beyond.

Lawn culture is a global phenomenon with between 70–75 per cent of urban green areas globally covered with them.[20][21] You can trace the ornamental lawn back to 17th century England[22] where rich folk surrounded their large estates with vast oceans of perfectly manicured green. It quickly became a status symbol: if you were cashed up you didn't have to grow your own food or graze livestock – you could just have a lawn for the pleasure of it. For the lower classes, a prim and proper lawn out the front of the house and a few roses became aspirational. (If you did have a food patch, you'd hide it behind your house so no one knew you had to grow food – imagine the shame!)

This narrative has trickled down the generations and we've embraced this colonial approach to landscaping, even where it's culturally and climatically out of place – such as in most of Australia, the driest inhabited continent on earth. In Perth, the annual volume of groundwater for irrigating public green spaces and private open spaces is around 140 gigalitres, enough to fill around 56,000 Olympic-sized swimming pools. In terms of actual cost to Perth's council, it's around $118 million each year for irrigating its public green grasses.[23] Imagine if your local council had that much money to spend on essential services (health, housing, education, childcare and so on) instead of watering the local lawn-scape?

Every year Americans use around 36 million kilograms of pesticides on their lawns.[24] The ramifications this has on the health of soil, water, insects, frogs and more can't be underestimated.

Considering all of this, and considering how anxious I feel in highly manicured gardens, you would think I'd be completely anti-lawn, and yet … I get it: there's something oddly attractive about big, lush lawns. One day I was on social media and a gardening account popped up as a suggested page to follow. It was for a lawn company – which isn't my thing – but the timelapse videos this bloke was putting up were super captivating. Over multiple days, I kept going back to his account to watch him manicure and tame unruly lawns into crisp green carpets. One time he even spray-painted a brown, dry lawn green. My favourite videos were of him cutting sharp edges: perfect straight lines or crisp curves with voiceovers explaining his technique and preferred tools. His voice was super calm, like someone leading a meditation class. As I watched his videos, my brain would go quiet just like in meditation. I was mesmerised.

My daughter teased me endlessly about this new habit so I eventually kicked it to the kerb, but I still think about it at least one to three times a week and she still teases me occasionally. Apparently this stuff is called 'lawn porn', and while I'm mostly avoiding it now, I think it might tell us something about our relationship with gardening. There must be something to analyse in my brain about why 'taming' a lawn makes me feel calm, while the highly manicured symmetry of French garden design makes me twitch. Maybe because when you mow an out-of-control lawn it looks like a problem has been solved. Or maybe because vast 'empty' green spaces relax my brain.

I wandered out to my garden to think on this more. Without a doubt, when we clip the small amount of lawn we do have I feel better about the garden. I get a similar feeling to when I sweep the floor in our house – like I'm on top of life (delusional, I know). But looking around our patch I can see the evolution of our gardening style over the years. What started as a more relaxed 'she'll be right' approach to gardening has evolved into an inclination for more structure. You'll see mass plantings that have crept in in recent years as I love the visual punch they throw, like the small yet impactful bank of Mexican sage bush (*Salvia leucantha*) we have. Its long purple flowers wave down the New Holland honeyeaters who hang onto those bopping purple spears for a feed – it's show-stopping beauty in action. The small hedge of red *Salvia greggii* hums with bees year-round and draws a line from our house to our much-adored greenhouse. It's a visual feast and guides both our feet and eyes through the space. My evergreen native hedges of sticky hopbush (*Dodonaea viscosa*) and Coastal Boobialla (*Myoporum insulare*) help hold parts of the garden together across our cool temperate seasons. I now have not one, but two electric hedge trimmers – a handheld one and another with a long arm so I can trim the maturing hedges more easily. Am I imposing my personal sense of order onto Nature – changing what she'd normally do by herself? Of course, but aren't we all – simply by existing? The flipside to this perspective is remembering that *we are Nature* and that we're simply finding our role within the garden ecosystem we're living within. I think the better question to ask is 'are we hurting Nature' with our gardening approach – if the answer's yes, then pivot until you're not.

Which brings me back to lawn culture – are we hurting Nature by establishing lawns all over the place? Unfortunately the answer is often yes. But are ornamental gardeners inherently hurting Nature? As long as they're leaving chemicals out of the picture and embracing diversity, then I say nah, they're just expressing their wonderful garden spirits – crisp straight lines and all.

On that note, sometimes in organic garden and permaculture circles I hear people say there are no straight lines in Nature, therefore any garden that has straight lines is out of sync with Nature and is doing a disservice. But I push back on that.

Humans are drawn to straight lines. You'll see us ignore curved paved pathways provided for us in parklands – instead we'll cut the most efficient path we can (a straight line) to get from point A to point B the quickest. In our own steep garden, we've excavated terraces into the slope, not perfectly straight – but they give that impression. They help us manage water and nutrient flow and create easy access. Plus our vegetables are planted in straight lines to make weeding, irrigating and crop rotation more functional.

Science and technology educator Luis Villazon explains that 'the reason we like straight lines is because of a fundamental property of the Universe – the shortest distance between two points is a straight line.' Nature, he points out, follows this same principle. 'Spiders, for example, make their webs by stretching silk strands across the shortest path.'[25]

Beauty is efficient, it's chaos, it's straight lines and it's spirals. Personally, I think as long as a garden approach isn't hurting Nature by polluting or contaminating it with harmful chemicals then it passes the beauty standard in that it fosters life, above and below ground. Just like Lou said earlier in this chapter, if a garden's healthy, it makes people feel something, and this is what makes it beautiful. That's the only beauty standard I'm interested in meeting.

For many years I watched a front garden just around the corner from me with great interest. It consisted of a finely manicured lawn and one apricot tree planted perfectly in the middle with a neat border around its base. The tree had been pruned incredibly formally with the canopy culminating in a perfectly flat top. (If you put a spirit level on it, it'd be dead level!) An older man lived there, and I regret that I never spoke to him. I'd see him out there tending to his lawn and pruning the apricot tree with a range of hand tools. One time I even saw him use what looked like small nail scissors. He was using them to trim the edges of the canopy to fit perfectly into the uniform shape he'd chosen.

At first I thought, 'That man is crazy.' But this feeling dissolved, morphed and evolved into something else over the years without me even noticing. Not until the house was sold did I pause and reflect. I'm not sure if the man died or simply moved, but the apricot tree started growing into a wild mess, which was beautiful in its own way. But I got a pang in my heart and I still get a stab of sadness every time I go past. I realised I loved witnessing the love the man had for his tree, for his lawn – the whole garden. He taught me something: that the love gardeners show their gardens transcends what that garden might actually look like. I loved his garden because of the way he loved it.

There are many possible approaches to gardening and garden design which ultimately reflects that individual's interpretation of beauty and what makes a good garden. But while all gardeners are different, the love that we have for our gardens is cut from the same cloth, or made in the same compost pile.

Changing beauty standards

Our concept of beauty can evolve over time. Mine has expanded to take in types of plants that I would never have considered in the past.

I drop in on my mate Jess to say g'day, to meet her new babe Hazel (who's bloody gorgeous) and catch up on life. As Jess is another avid gardener, it only takes us 4.5 minutes to stop talking about Hazel and start talking about gardens. We do this to the soundscape of Hazel suckling and snorting away, guzzling milk from Jess's boob.

Jess bought a house in the suburbs of Nipaluna/Hobart with her partner, George, five years earlier. It came with a bank of agapanthus they're learning to live with and a bunch of roses they promptly removed to make way for a large productive garden.

But years later, to her surprise, she had a moment of becoming what she calls 'rose-curious'. On a recent nursery trip she came home with a rose by the name of Jude the Obscure: a pale apricot shrub rose with large flowers. Both Jess and I could once be described as strictly functional growers (food or nothing). But it seems like we're now simultaneously sliding down the fun and wonderful slippery slope of falling in love with most plants. While Jess is geeking out on roses, I recently became 'crepe myrtle curious' (*Lagerstroemia indica*) and am researching the exact species I want to plant near our front gate to be our property's official 'welcome tree'. It needs to be the right shade of pink to 'speak to my pink house' and it needs to be the right form so it's tall, but not too tall. And the bark patterns need to be particularly stunning (when it's both wet or dry) so that even through its deciduous time in winter (where it drops its leaves) it screams beauty and makes us pause to admire it. Younger me would be shocked at planting something so ornamental. Older Hannah is like, 'Chill, mate, I'm just doing anything and everything I can to foster love and life, both in and out of the garden.' It just so happens that including flowering plants in my garden that match my pink house and my pink hair is one way of doing this!

I ask Jess why she gardens:

For the love of plants. Every time you meet a new one, it's a whole world! I like finding out where they're from, how did they get here, do they even like it here? I guess I've always loved learning and if you want to spend your whole life learning then plants are your things because you'll never cover all of them, you'll never know all of them intimately. That's why this garden is always a bit wild but never feels big enough. George thinks we can't manage more space than this. *But I need more space for all my friends!* I don't have enough space! And it's why my garden will never look like the landscape design of my dreams: because I'm such a 'one of everything' [kind of gardener], I want to know what they all look like.

We both agree that there's a level of intimacy and plant knowledge that you can only get once you've lived and grown with plants. They do become your friends.

Jess records all the information she gathers about her plants/friends in an Excel spreadsheet (it's a very big spreadsheet). She's excited to continue learning, to continue falling in love with new types of plants, and to continue expanding her ideas of beauty in gardening.

I feel very confident that I'll spend the rest of my life sniffing around plants. That's part of the joy of meeting other gardeners, if you catch that bug: if it speaks to you in some way, you see how it never goes away. You don't lose it, you don't hear, 'Oh, I was a gardener for 5 years and then I got over it.'

Beauty is in our nature

Sally Ives lives just outside Cygnet in southern Lutruwita/Tasmania. I met Sally while filming with her for *Gardening Australia*. Sally and her partner, Mike, moved onto 5 acres, built a house and transformed one acre of paddock into a stunning home garden that's a living rainbow. There are sploshes of colour everywhere among a predominately perennial garden that includes ornamentals, natives and edibles. Lettuce is growing up between the pavers, native cushion bush (*Leucophyta brownii*) hugs the stone steps and roses wrap around the house. It's all love and eye candy.

Sally was born in 1968 in Changping District in Beijing. At ten months old, she went to live with her grandparents (as was, and still is, common practice) in Laiguangying Township, about 25 kilometres northeast of Tiananmen Square. The area was mainly farming land until the 90s. The village where Sally grew up was surrounded by fields of rice, wheat and maize, alongside crops such as peanuts, sweet potatoes and Chinese cabbage.

> The government owns all the land in China. My grandad and my mum's two brothers all had jobs but my grandma and my uncles' wives were all farmers. How it worked was that farmers in the village all worked in the field together. A record was kept to show how many days each farmer worked. At the end of the year they would be given a share of the crop (mainly maize with a little bit of rice and wheat) according to how many days they worked.
>
> Our life in those days was very basic although we never went hungry or cold. Maize flour was our main carbohydrate. It was usually made into pancakes or buns or porridge. We didn't have much but it was a free and happy childhood, very well cared for by our very loving yet strict grandparents.

Sally lived with her grandparents until she was eleven when she returned to live with her parents to access better schooling. But before then her childhood, and her understanding of gardening, was shaped by her grandparents. While her grandparents' style of gardening was primarily for survival, her grandmother still grew plants for beauty as well.

Most things my grandma grew were of course edible but the

few ornamental plants I remember we had in the courtyard were honeysuckle, star jasmine, basil, fuchsia and red impatiens.

Honeysuckle and star jasmine filled the courtyard with fragrance. I don't remember we ever ate basil but I do remember my grandma sometimes put a honeysuckle or jasmine flower or a little sprig of basil on her ear. I assume they were her perfume. She also sometimes put a fuchsia flower on her or my ear.

It was the red impatiens (it is called nail grass in Chinese) which she picked the petals and turned them into a paste then covered her nails with the paste. I seem to remember she added some salt to the paste. She did it for me too but you need to stay still for quite a while for the colour to set on the nails. I never had the patience.

Life was primitive for my grandma and growing veggies was part of the survival for her but she certainly still had the love for the simple but truly beautiful things in life.

Even when people *have to* grow food, they sometimes find themselves growing the unnecessary things to bring beauty and joy into their lives. I asked Sally what her grandmother would think of her current garden which is a cacophony of life and colour.

There is virtually a forty-year gap between the days when I gardened with my grandma and us starting here on a blank canvas in 2015 when I think the seed my grandma sowed that many years ago finally sprouted. Ever since I just can't stop. It has become an incurable obsession and addiction, one I am proud of. I feel extremely grateful that I now have the time and space to grow many beautiful things, both edibles and ornamentals.

I think my grandma would be super proud of me if she knew

how much I am growing now ... How I wish I could have a little stroll with her in my garden with a cup of jasmine tea. She probably could not stop picking flowers though. I reckon she would love my hidcote lavender and rose geraniums.

Post filming, we were scrambling through her garden, taking cuttings of salvias and succulents for me to take home for my own garden. Sally told me that growing ornamental plants is like growing food for your soul. I took the bunches of cuttings into my arms and my whole heart lit up with the fact that I was cradling at least thirty new plants! It's a thrill that all gardeners understand.

While our bodies thrive on produce grown in healthy soils, our souls blossom when exposed to diverse expressions of love and joy — of which flowers are one of the most powerful symbols. I went home and turned the cuttings into dozens of new plants, thinking of Sally and her grandmother the whole time. How gardening has a habit of flowing through generations, across cultures and countries, finding a way to help us survive, but also thrive in the beauty of it all

For creativity

Bogged
down, heart
drowning
Woosh, a bird
flies through
the trees
I gasp with
delight

The type of work I do includes writing, TV presenting, education, performance, community projects, project management, gardening and design. When people ask me 'What do you do for work?' I have to brace myself before embarking on a long-winded explanation. When our daughter was in grade two, a lot of the parents were invited to come and chat to the class about what type of work they did in the world to spark the kids' interest. I never ended up going as we couldn't work out what to say!

But I love that about my work life: every day is different and is reliant on me bringing my creativity to the table to make things work. Because creativity has a home everywhere with everyone – it's the juice, the spice, the spark that morphs into whatever you need it to be to make meaningful things happen. It's also a force that drives me to try to be more than I am, which means I'm always out of my comfort zone with at least one project making me feel 'a bit sick' – but I'd choose that feeling over the opposite any day. Because I've learned that when I'm comfortable, I feel wildly underutilised and that's my absolute least favourite feeling.

One project that made me feel sick for over a year was developing a cabaret about climate justice with the biennial arts festival Ten Days on the Island. Not being formally trained in the arts I was happily shocked when they invited me to be one of their guest creatives for this amazing festival. I quickly said yes before they changed their minds and promised myself I'd work out the details later.

The foundation of my art offering came quickly and was based around exploring climate justice in a fun and solutions-oriented way that would engage and inspire people. My problem was, how?

And then one day, while struggling with this question and talking to my office wall to see if it had any ideas, I pulled on my sneakers and strolled through my garden, and then went for a run in my local bush. While jumping over rocks and huffing and puffing to the loud soundtrack of 'Sweet Dreams' by the Eurythmics, I had a moment of inspiration. *It was obvious!* The project had to be a musical or cabaret. People singing and acting freely and outrageously in a room together is all joy and a wonderful way to connect. I firmly believe we need more of this vibe when talking about climate solutions. In a flash I could see smiling faces, dancing, giant cardboard trees and vegetable props, colour, loud music, singing, joy and connection.

The thing about inspiration and creativity is that it's not always grounded in reality. Me developing a cabaret was like Beyoncé deciding to become a goat farmer. Had I ever created a cabaret before? No. Could I sing? Not very well. Did I have any acting experience? Zero.

And so proceeded months of struggle as I tried to develop my idea. But without fail, a trip to my garden or a brisk walk or run in the local bush pulled me back to a place of free-flowing creativity where I was able to get out of my own way and just let it happen. Despite lacking the talent required for a cabaret, inspiration was screaming at me, 'You gotta do this, Hannah' and the garden (and Nature) helped let that inspiration in. I had a strong feeling deep in my bones that by collaborating with some amazing professionals,[26] bringing all my goodness and working my arse off it was going to be amazing. And you know what? It was beyond magic.

I called it Time Rebel, a term coined by social philosopher Roman Krznaric (who gave his blessing for me to use it) which describes someone who works towards intergenerational justice (more on that later). Time Rebel was a one-woman show consisting of me in my wedding dress, telling a story of what climate justice can look like. The performance also included large community choirs in each of the places we performed the show in. It was an enormous challenge for me and I would never have had the guts or gumption to even attempt it if it wasn't for my strong belief that creativity can be the foundation for real, progressive change.

And where did that inspiration and creativity stem from? My garden and the local bush (and Eurythmics).

Nature loves art, and vice versa

For as long as I can remember I've believed that Nature (in all its forms) and creativity (in all its forms) are best friends. Personally, I've found that Nature helps me think and act better as it reminds me who I am: not overly special, but also part of the most magical and interconnected thing imaginable: life!

Barcelona's famous architect Antoni Gaudi said, 'Anything created by human beings is already in the great book of nature.' Looking at

Gaudi's work, you can see nature's the inspiration shining through. Buildings are curved, spirals are common, colour is everywhere in the form of bold mosaic tiles, and windows are rainbow stained glass. It's a beautiful and bold rebellion against the architectural norms both then and now. Bob Brown extends this thinking: 'It's true, take away Nature and we take away our basic source of inspiration and creativity.'

Author Tim Winton's writing is so often wrapped in and around Nature: 'I think anyone who's read my books will already know that nature is a central character in most of my stories. And the fate of the natural world has become more and more of a preoccupation over time.'

When I ask Tim if the garden helps his creative process he explains, 'Going out into the garden can be a circuit breaker, a change of tone, a reset. Unless there's a king brown [snake] in the tomato house – then the indoors looks just fine!'

It's been proven multiple times over that spending time in Nature can help increase your ability to hold attention to a task, increase creativity, make you feel happy and decrease stress.[27] The more we can integrate gardens and Nature into our lives and creative practice the better. There is nothing to lose and everything to gain.

When I interviewed award-winning musician and author Clare Bowditch, she explained how she draws on gardens and Nature in her creative work:

There's always references to nature in there. But what I really draw from is the lessons and creativity a garden can give us and applying them back to my creative work. So you only have to make the smallest effort and the creativity of nature will meet you halfway there and then some. That it doesn't abandon you, that it's ever present, that it's often sitting there waiting to be enjoyed and made use of and again back to that generosity. So I think I use the garden often as a metaphor in the creative process.

Her garden is also central to her home. As we spoke online, Clare flipped her screen and showed me how her current home renovation is completely centred around their old olive tree that was there when they moved in. When you step through the front door you see straight down a long hallway through a glass wall looking out to their garden with this old, gnarly olive tree perfectly framed by the window. It made me gasp with delight. What a sight to come home to!

After swooning over her olive tree, Clare and I began talking deep with one another. We talked about how to be in the world, how to keep going among all the shit that is human nature. We talked about how to do meaningful work that is worthy of sharing with the world, despite all the 'what's the point?' feelings.

After opening up, Clare reflected, 'I didn't even know that I was thinking any of this until I started walking around my garden.' Gardens can do that to us. They can open us up without us even noticing, and sometimes, we manage to capture snippets of insights and clarity for how to be or how we already are and remember to embrace that. At the end of our chat, I blew Clare air kisses through the computer screen, grateful to her for sharing her thoughts with me and sharing her creativity with the world.

Brenna and Charlie

Brenna Quinlan and Charlie Mcgee live in southwest Western Australia in a little town called Denmark, around 4.5 hours south of Boorloo/ Perth. They're both incredible artists and musicians. But it was through permaculture[28] work that I came to know them and insisted on being friends with them. They are heart-powered, hardworking people and I'm a big fan of both their spirits and art. It's amazing to see how they combine Nature and creativity. Charlie, a songwriter and musician, has a band called Formidable Vegetable Sound System that sparks inspiration towards earth-based regenerative culture and community. He told me: 'When we started writing songs about permaculture principles (which is one of the nerdiest things anyone's ever done with music), it's evolved. We do everything from electronic dance music, DJ-ing, to children's music projects playing at schools and in festivals too. You'll also find us hosting community garden parties. Wherever we can find a niche to spread that message in whatever form it takes is what we do.'

I visited Charlie and Brenna after they moved into a strawbale house they've been building for three years (great timing on my behalf!). They set me up in their strawbale studio and I spent almost a week catching up with them while I worked on this book and other projects. Among the work, I jumped in the ocean and followed them to their community events. It was like being on a creative retreat.

One arvo we sat down in their loungeroom, cuppa in hand, so I could interview them for this book. I'm always fascinated by creatives who are so prolific with their work. I wanted to know what helps them get out of any creative slumps they experience and what inspires them to keep creating.

For Brenna it's all about having an active, daily outdoors lifestyle where the garden is a source of inspiration:

> Having our house face our garden is an active design choice. We all need time when our brains are at rest or at a different level, so if we like thinking or creating or stretching it in other ways,

that's good, and that needs to be balanced by some sort of brain relaxation state. And for me I can get decent exercise while I'm running around the garden while my brain is really calm and that balances the other side of my life which can be pretty intense.

The garden is central to Charlie's life as well:

I think you can have some pretty profound insights into the universe from the garden – you can just go as deep as you want. Just through doing something like composting and contemplating what's going on, a world explodes in your brain. And that's the inspiration for most of our art. Cause we'll be doing something as simple as chucking some weeds on a compost heap and then suddenly we're thinking about the soil food web, reading books about it and getting experience of it in real life and then synthesising that into music and art and it's just another element of those connections in the garden.

Sitting at their dining table I look straight out onto their extensive vegetable garden that's been built into the gentle slope with a series of terraces. It spreads along the full length of the house, dominating the view from every window. Sheets of recycled corrugated iron have been used for retaining walls and edible borage, nasturtium and calendula flowers weave themselves through the too-abundant zucchini bushes and pumpkin vines.

Over the years, Brenna and Charlie have often had friends and volunteers helping in their garden or on their house build which has given them ample opportunity to connect with wildly diverse folks, creating even more opportunities for creativity and inspiration. 'The more connections I have with people who are excited about growing, soil or plants [the more I hear people's different perspectives] so the more fodder I have for my 'ideas book' and they filter through into my drawing,' says Brenna. Charlie sums it up perfectly: 'While they're harvesting peas, you're harvesting art!'

For Brenna and Charlie gardening fuels and inspires them, keeping them grounded in their 'why' while they also use it as a tool for change — both for themselves and others.

The farmer in the suburbs

And then there's my dad. He's over eighty now. He says he gardens because it's 'creative — a portrayal of life and beauty'. Getting to know him as an adult and looking back, I can see how the land and gardening has shaped his whole life.

Before I was born, my parents and their growing family had moved all over Australia, living in caravans, bush shacks and semi-communal open houses that ran along Catholic worker principles. There was lots of social justice activism and people coming and going. But with an increasing number of kids arriving (I was number five), communal living wasn't fitting the bill. The story goes that when my mum was heavily pregnant with me she cracked the shits after a failed attempt at a communal living arrangement and that's what spurred the move to the big city (aka Meanjin/Brisbane).

To say Dad was miserable in the city is a wild understatement. I grew up thinking my dad was pretty darn angry at the world and I think he probably was. Our house was a sprawling Queenslander with an old mechanic's workshop in the backyard — a far cry from the bush shacks my dad had previously called home. A wannabe farmer, one of dad's coping mechanisms was to transform our quarter acre property into a herb nursery which eventually expanded into the garden next door when Mum and he managed to buy that house.

Then my dad's mum moved across the road and he was like, 'Hey, you've got a backyard too!' That's how he ended up with around half an acre of herb nursery in the middle of West End. I have vivid memories of Dad walking up and down the street with his wheelbarrow, carting herbs back and forth between his patches of nursery. It was pretty cool really and it gave me an innate understanding that cityscapes are still landscapes, and an appreciation of urban agriculture. While still living there, Dad wrote about his time in Kurilpa/West End:

> The challenge was to make a garden and a plant nursery from a mechanic's workshop and a yard of bitumen, oil and battery acid ingrained clay and shale intermixed with broken glass and metal. Where there was one tree and no soil I made a series of gardens, some now with 20 metre gum trees with understory, fruit trees, poultry and bird aviaries and a nursery business that provided about half our income. Where there had been just sparrows and starlings I have recorded thirty-three species of native birds, fifteen species of butterflies, four of frogs and I have never been sure of the reptile numbers due to the variety of legless lizards that emerge when working the soil. Recently a carpet python entered this 'yard' and we found it draped over one of the aviaries in pursuit of the birds within.

My memories of that home are of a beautiful garden full of life. There was no sign of the old mechanics yard – Dad worked wonders in and on that place.

As well as being a super functional gardener in those years (it was his full-time job for over eighteen years), he was also an incredibly creative one. Dad was always collecting old bits of timber, rusty wire and dead pieces of machinery and arranging them in some abstract form to hang in and on our house or place around the garden. I call it agricultural art. It was super normal to see him wrap rusty barbed wire around an old bit of timber and then hang it in our hallway. Friends who came over for the first time would be like 'What and why is that?' And I'd be like, 'Oh, that's just Dad.'

Gardening and farming not only informs Dad's art practice, it *is* his art practice. He built a large pergola structure then trained rampant pumpkins over the top (we called it the Pumpkin House). Each season the pumpkins would create this shady edible oasis with long fruits hanging down, like old stretchy boobs. He'd create different garden rooms: one for a campfire, another little pocket flanked by gumtrees (his beer-drinking spot), another for the chook yard and one for the trampoline. And all around this was the herb nursery plus some magnificent fruit and nut trees.

After Mum died, he eventually moved to 40 acres of degraded, scrubby farm land west of Meanjin/Brisbane. Over eighteen years he regenerated it into a truly beautiful forested and grassed landscape and did some bloody beautiful landscaping with sculptures everywhere. And then he followed three of us kids to Lutruwita/ Tasmania where he now lives – a move of necessity as old age crept in. Devastatingly, he had to leave behind SO MUCH timber, tools and general useful things – you could see it hurt his heart. But it simply wasn't practical to move it across the country and it definitely wouldn't fit on his new urban home of 600 square metres. To try to ease the sense of loss and shock, I borrowed a friend's car and picked up a load of old logs that people were throwing out. I delivered them to Dad's place and his whole face lit up. Nothing like some structural organic matter to make my dad smile. He placed them among his freshly landscaped garden to give some sense of Nature to his new urban life. No matter where my dad finds himself, whether it's a remote bush shack or a block of land in the inner city, he'll find a way to transform the space into a gardener's dream. He'll imbue the space with his own unique spark and love of Nature, inspiring not only himself but anyone lucky enough to pass through his garden galaxy.

Reigniting the spark

My very beautiful husband, Anton, had a rough patch: multiple years of enormous work focused on climate action initiatives that he gave his whole head and heart to and which culminated in a shit storm of stress. While he passionately believed in the work, he gradually sacrificed his health to it – something I don't recommend. This chapter of life culminated in a broken hip while skateboarding (trying to relieve some of that stress), an emergency operation to screw it all back together and three solid months of either lying down in bed or hobbling around on crutches which ultimately meant he decided to step back from his work to recover. It wasn't an overly cheery time in our lives. Our friends and community rallied around us, which I'm forever grateful for, but stress is a magnificent breeding ground for all sorts of unwanted weeds to flourish – weeds that have deep tap roots that'll rip through your head and heart if you're not careful. All of which is to say that Anton was in the deep dumps. We made the call for him to take a long sabbatical to heal and to heal properly – inside and out.

At the time of writing we've just passed fifteen years of loving each other and while we've experienced ups and downs (mostly stuff like I want goats, he's not so keen etc.) there's always been a foundation of ease wrapped around our love. But the few years leading up to the hip break were heart-achingly hard, not for the lack of love but for the abundance of stress.

Why am I telling you all this? Faced with a gorgeous husband who had forgotten himself, whose spark was fizzing out, who was losing inspiration, I was very much keen to help. One of the ways I tried in that three-month period was to propose we do a rather massive mosaic project in the garden, covering a 15 by 2 metre retaining wall in smashed tiles. It was a huge amount of work requiring patience and a lot of sit-down time (something Anton had in abundance that summer). Halfway through we realised we were basically doing some version of unofficial art therapy. We had subconsciously created a project that had a meaningful purpose, that allowed him to spend hours outside in the garden and that had the opportunity for connection. This last point came about with friends and family joining in and spending hours together smashing tiles and then piecing them back together again. And how does the wall look now? Fucking stunning! It's bold yellow and white stripes with black grout tying it together. It's all spunk and love.

And then, you know what he did? Having never welded before he borrowed a mate's welder (thanks DC) and welded me a life size, perfectly proportioned unicorn sculpture for our garden out of scrap metal from the local tip shop.

But he didn't stop there. He went and built us the greenhouse of our dreams with a recycled brick base, local hardwood timber and old windows from our home renovation we'd been saving behind the shed for years. It looks like something from a fairy tale. My heart swelled seeing his spark coming back. I'll let Anton tell you in his own words:

Last year was pretty rough. I think [gardening] did help but it's probably more the environment – rather than the actual gardening. I've really enjoyed the craft projects in the garden. It was a process starting from where I couldn't walk – so I'd sit on the stool and glue the little things to the wall [to make the mosaic]. And then the unicorn and then, as my strength built up, being able to do bigger and better things … and now we get to sit in this little church of a greenhouse.

And we do sit in the greenhouse, watching our goats doing goaty things through the window, happy dog on my lap, our tomatoes growing – it's all very dreamy. The word 'grateful' feels wildly inadequate for both the greenhouse and a healthy husband.

Throughout this time his hip healed like actual bloody magic. He took up surfing again and wrestling with our daughter, his eyes regained their sparkle, he gave himself a mohawk (short lived due to our daughter's horror), he started having new ideas and wondering about future fun adventures and possibilities. I have deep-gut relief that my beautiful husband has remembered himself. I put his recovery down to three key things that we were able to give him: time, gardening and creativity.

Watching Anton's recovery cemented something in my mind that I had always suspected: gardening and Nature can inspire us, heal us and help creativity flow through us. They're intrinsically linked, and I never want to live without them.

- 'Gardening has enriched my life showing me daily glimpses of resilience, beauty, and love, colour, joy, peace, calm and acceptance. It nurtures creativity, problem solving, humour and pride. Nature taught me to listen deeply and feel grateful for every win and challenge life brings. Nature shows up daily and so do I.' **Alli Yacoumis**

- 'Visually very beautiful, colour, form, texture. Also another form of creativity … making a space and place. Connected to bush around us. Memorial. Celebration. A form of miracle.' **Sarah**

- 'Many non-interested people end up enjoying gardening. Instant gratification/slow rewards and creativity.' **Claire Artuso**

- 'My mind is soothed most when I am in contact with my garden and the soil. It allows creativity and art.' **Lara T**

- 'It's a place of solace. Theres no fear, no negativity, just pure joy and creativity.' **Leah Edwards**

- 'It is my sanity and my spirituality. Gardening is a relationship with life and all it creates and sustains. To be reminded of the vast, intricate and wonderful life source I'm encased by and a part of is awe inspiring.' **Jade P**

For our bodies

Carries me
always
Strong arms
hug my family
I love my body

I grew up eating incredibly healthy food – lots of wholefoods, veggies, eggs from our backyard chickens, herbs, fruit and greens from the garden. We ate mostly vegetarian meals with occasional meat and the rule was that you had to eat your salad before you got dinner. There were no regular treats at all. While my friends had Monte Carlo biscuits and chocolate snacks, I'd raid the carob powder jar, eating it by the spoonful to get a sweetness hit (but when Mum found out she stopped buying it). Sometimes we'd be extra sneaky and make toast with the wholemeal bread, lather it with Nuttelex margarine (this was the time when butter was meant to be bad for you) and sprinkle brown sugar and cinnamon onto it. Heaven!

On our birthdays and special occasions, Dad would make what he called the Plain Cake and decorate it with edible flowers from the garden. It was a basic cake with wholemeal flour, milk, brown sugar, eggs and a teaspoon of vanilla essence as the main flavour. We'd line up to lick the bowl, and when he was feeling generous he'd leave extra mixture for us to clean up with our sticky fingers. It was hard to get much in the way of treats in my childhood! Even the small primary school I went to banned lollies. It was bloody agony as a kid.

While initially deeply resentful, I ended up appreciating and adopting this approach to food because my body felt good: strong, energetic and clean. These days with my own little family I take a similar approach to Mum and Dad. However, my personal challenge is that my husband is half Swedish and grew up with the understanding that butter, cheese, bread and baked sweet things with white flour and sugar is of the utmost cultural importance and a human right. Our daughter prefers it when he cooks … weird. But even among the cakes and slabs of butter on bread, our large edible garden and the seasons determine the bulk of what we eat.

What we put into our bodies is so important. I'm approximately 200 per cent more relaxed about food than my parents were. There's chocolate in our house, our daughter has treats more often than I care to admit and at ten years old knows how to make cakes and biscuits by heart (she had that sorted by age seven). I'm mostly okay with it because she still reaches for those homegrown carrots, still knows that to be healthy and strong she's gotta get those greens into her. With my parenting hat on, it's satisfying (and relieving) to see that it's already engrained into her. And I sigh with relief when our daughter, Frida Maria, occasionally says, 'You know what? I just need some fresh carrots and greens from the garden, Mama.'

Dr Norman Swan said: 'If we all eat more plants and far less meat, we'd live longer healthier lives, make farming more sustainable, and help to mitigate climate change and resource scarcity leading to conflict.'[29]

There's a lot to unpack in that one sentence, but let's start with the first six words: 'If we all eat more plants'. Sounds simple, but what if those plants are lacking essential nutrients?

Between 1950 and 1999 an American study led by Dr Donald David from the University of Texas recorded a decline in nutrition across forty-three food crops. These nutrients included protein, calcium, phosphorus, iron, riboflavin and ascorbic acid. The declines raised questions about how modern agriculture practices affected food crops. Davis concluded that:

> … the most likely explanation was changes in cultivated varieties used today compared to 50 years ago … During those 50 years, there have been intensive efforts to breed new varieties that have greater yield, resistance to pests, or adaptability to different climates. But the dominant effort is for higher yields. Emerging evidence suggests that when you select for yield, crops grow bigger and faster, but they don't necessarily have the ability to make or uptake nutrients at the same, faster rate.[30]

So, what was going on? In short, it's the massive changes we've seen in agriculture. Let's take a look at the green revolution (GR) which ran from 1950 into the 1980s, and which was tasked with solving world hunger. American agronomist Norman Ernest Borlaug is known as the godfather of the GR and was awarded a Nobel Peace Prize in 1970 for his work in this area. During thirty-plus years the GR was responsible for increasing world grain production (in particular wheat and rice) by a mind-boggling 160 per cent, specifically in Latin America and India.[31] [32]

It all started when Borlaug developed a robust, disease-resistant dwarf strain of wheat that was able to produce more food per plant. He dramatically increased crop productivity and, once these new varieties were introduced, researchers saw a decrease in malnutrition in those areas.[33]

But despite making bigger yields of wheat per plant, the levels of nutrients per plant did not increase in the same way. Professor Steve McGrath, who specialises in soil and plant science at Rothamsted Research in the United Kingdom, explains:

> What we end up with is a scenario where, while the nutrients remain at the same level in a single wheat kernel, the starch is up two or three-fold. This means that once the wheat is processed into flour you get a dilution effect. The ratio of carbohydrates to nutrients is down.[34]

The dilution effect is what you get when you breed a plant to increase in size, but not to increase its nutrient content. Essentially, you end up with more volume of food (yay) but with less nutrients (boo) as those nutrients have been spread across a greater volume of food. This creates something called 'hidden hunger' which refers to food that is calorie-rich but nutrient-poor. So, you could actually be a healthy weight or even obese but be nutritionally hungry.[35]

Other unintended consequences of the GR include 'loss of biodiversity, the lowering of the water table, increased salinization, an increased use of pesticides (leaving residuals in the environment), and increased rural inequalities'.[36] The last of these is mainly due to the inability of poor farmers to afford the ongoing costs of buying seed and fertilisers required for this type of farming to actually work.

This is a long way of saying that the nutritional quality of fresh food we eat is (a) important for our personal health, (b) compromised by conventional agriculture, and (c) makes up another key reason for why people grow food, specifically so they can grow quality, nutrient-dense food for themselves.

- '[I garden] to create a good relationship with food and nature for my children.' **Anonymous**
- 'I get a lot of joy from growing nutritious, chemical-free food. It is also really good for my physical and mental health.' **Glenyse T**
- 'As I reached my forties the idea of nourishing my body (a body that has fought and won the battle against breast cancer) with produce I have grown excites me.' **Cheyenne Johnson**
- 'Knowing the provenance of our food is really important – and when it comes from my garden there are countless benefits for health, wealth, community and climate.' **Veronika Barry**

Sadly, there are countless stories across the world of certain agricultural chemicals being linked to devastating environmental and human health outcomes, especially for farmers. One example is a story covered by ABC TV's *Landline* focusing on a cluster of Australian farmers in Victoria all experiencing Parkinson's disease. Research shows that there is a strong possibility of it being linked to using a chemical known as paraquat.[37]

Paraquat is the active ingredient in 141 products in Australia with more than 10 million kilograms purchased in Australia alone in the 2023/24 financial year. Independent studies show that farmers using it are 2.5 times more likely to have symptoms of Parkinson's.

A company called Syngenta is the original manufacturer. They have consistently stated that their scientists are confident there's no link between paraquat and Parkinson's. However, numerous independent scientists disagree. ABC researchers found twenty-eight peer reviewed studies over the past two decades that found that paraquat induces one or more of the features of Parkinson's.

'I'd say that farmers are overly represented in the cohort of patients I see with Parkinson's disease,' said Dr Wesley Thevathasan, a neurologist based in Melbourne. 'And this is not surprising because we know that rural living and potential exposure to pesticides is a likely risk factor for developing the condition. All sorts of agents have been implicated, but the evidence is strongest for paraquat.'[38]

Landline also reported that '67 countries have banned paraquat due to its toxicity … It's prohibited in the UK, China and the EU. But in Australia, demand for the chemical is as strong as ever.'

This is just one of the reasons why we're seeing interest in organic, regenerative food production increase. Growers and eaters simply want to be safe and healthy with what they put in their bodies. Is that too much to ask?

Quite recently, organic food was simply called 'food' as no chemical fertilisers were used. This only changed after World War II when governments realised they could use the leftover ammonium nitrate, which was originally designed for warfare explosives, as a nitrogen fertiliser for agricultural crops.[39] The BOOM of war explosives was replaced with the BOOM of conventional agriculture. Suddenly we saw the rise of larger farms, monoculture crops and the increased use of other pesticides, herbicides and fungicides that this style of farming leans on to succeed.

It could be seen as noble to take something that was designed to harm or kill and repurpose it with the aim of helping to feed people.

And I do believe that good intentions were the driving force. But you could also say there's something philosophically sad about transitioning ingredients meant for warfare into our precious food system. The stuff that's meant to nourish us and keep us alive is being sprayed with the stuff that was once used to kill people. I struggle to make it feel right.

When I was talking with Australian author Bruce Pascoe he made the point that 'if you're growing plants and eating your own plants, you'll make sure that the plant you're going to eat is going to be healthy. You'll make sure that there's no poisons applied … so the closer we can have contact to our food the better it's going to be'.

Gardening can do exactly that: ensure a closer connection with the food we eat. And it could even lead to a deeper appreciation of what we all depend on: the ground beneath our feet being healthy, so that the food we grow can be healthy, and we can be healthy too.

Nature's pharmacy

Gardening has been part of my preventative and responsive medicine cabinet. The daily activities of 'extreme gardening', as I call it, on our steep 30-degree slope help keep my body limber and strong. But as well as all the physical exercise that gardening requires, food gardening can deliver additional benefits for our health and wellbeing.

As long as gardening and foraging has existed, humans have used plants for all sorts of physical benefits including sourcing a range of plant-based medicines to stay healthy or to get healthy. For many centuries plants and organic materials were the only options and to this day 'around 40 per cent of pharmaceutical products draw from nature and traditional knowledge, including landmark drugs: aspirin, artemisinin, and childhood cancer treatments'.[40] Chinese medicine, naturopathy, herbal remedies, homeopathy and Indigenous traditional medicines across the globe all have ancient roots as well as modern relevance.

After working unsuccessfully for years on a cure for malaria, it wasn't until Chinese scientist Tu Youyou turned to traditional Chinese medical documents that she cracked the code. She found a reference to sweet wormwood (*Artemisia annua*) being used to treat fevers. By isolating an active compound called artemisinin in sweet wormwood Tu Youyou and her team found the most effective form of treating malaria and were able to save millions of lives. In 2015, Tu Youyou was awarded the Nobel Prize in Physiology or Medicine for her work on malaria. What a legend.

I didn't realise that the foundation of aspirin, now one of the most-used drugs in the world, is willow bark (*Salix alba vulgaris*). Research shows that the Sumerians and Egyptians used bark from the willow tree over 3500 years ago 'as a pain reliever and an anti-inflammatory'.[41] In ancient Greece, willow bark was used to aid women giving birth to help reduce the pain and for other folks suffering with fevers.

Meanwhile, childhood cancer drugs vinblastine and vincristine are sourced from the Madagascar periwinkle plant (*Catharanthus roseus*) and can be found referenced in traditional Chinese medicine, Mesopotamian folklore and the Indian Ayurveda system. And then there's foxglove (*Digitalis purpurea*) and hawthorn (*Crataegus monogyna*) which can be used to address hypertension and cardiovascular disease. Star anise (*Illicium verum*) provides something called shikimic acid that's used in Tamiflu, a medication that blocks the actions of influenza A and B in the body. And the wild Mexican yam (*Dioscorea villosa*) produces norethindrone, an active ingredient in contraceptive pills.[42] How cool are plants?!

Like a lot of people, I grew up with plant medicine being a normal part of my sickness experience. If I had a cold, it'd be hot drinks of lemon and ginger and the dreaded 'green drink'. The green drink was a freshly made juice with apples as the base but then it had loads of freshly picked leaves of dandelion[43] (*Taraxacum officinale*) and comfrey (*Symphytum officinale*). It actually tasted quite nice (thanks to all the apples) but I dreaded it because it was so bloody effective. I knew that if I drank it I'd get better and have to go back to school sooner than I would have liked.

Just a quick note on comfrey. It's commonly used topically as a poultice or pre-made ointment (from the leaf or root) to treat bruises, sprains and broken bones. If you look through historical records you'll see it's earned itself nicknames like knitbone and boneset because – you guessed it – it has a reputation as being an effective herb to help mend broken bones.

In the 1600s, Nicholas Culpeper, an English botanist, herbalist, physician and astrologer, mentioned comfrey in his book *The English Physician*. Culpeper helped poor people grow what they needed medicinally instead of buying overpriced remedies from doctors. He recommended comfrey for both external and internal use. The internal use was said to help cure 'gastritis, peptic ulcers, cough remedies … and rheumatism, pleurisy, bronchitis, diarrhoea and tumours'.[44]

But these days it's no longer recommended for internal consumption in any capacity due to the risk of ingesting potentially toxic pyrrolizidine alkaloids which can damage your liver. So, to be very clear, just because I grew up on the green drink as being the annoyingly effective medicine drink, doesn't mean I'm recommending it to you all. Also, my liver is 100 per cent fine, thanks for asking.

You might have heard the popular saying that food is medicine, alluding to the fact that if you eat nutrient-dense food you'll be better off for it. But did you know that gardening and Nature are increasingly being prescribed by doctors to treat both physical and mental ailments?

Researchers have found: 'Nature prescribing is likely to increase physical activity and improve mental and cardiovascular health outcomes. Nature prescribing can be incorporated into prevention programs, as well as chronic disease and mental health management in general practice.'[45]

Often us humans will intuitively do a touch of 'nature prescribing' ourselves. While processing my mum's death when I was eighteen, I gardened, WWOOFed[46] and bushwalked across Australia. When dealing with a soul-shaking heartbreak in my twenties, I grew the best eggplants in my life due to obsessively gardening. The 'dark empty' that is postpartum depression led to some wild productivity in our home garden. The destabilising world of hormonal changes with perimenopause that started disturbingly early in my mid-thirties resulted in community and home projects with food and wellbeing at their heart. And learning to live with premenstrual dysphoric disorder (PMDD) which delivers almost-crippling anxiety and chronic migraines in overwhelming and too-regular waves since my early thirties has manifested in evolving my garden to include more non-edible plants to create some calm and peace in my life. The garden has been a literal lifeline for me, propping me up with promises of seeds sprouting, trees fruiting and flowers blooming.

In time I found the right combination of life changes and medication to help manage my symptoms, but it took eight long years and too many doctors who didn't believe my symptoms were real, or who simply couldn't find a solution. It's worth pointing out, though, that without fail, all the best doctors and specialists I saw encouraged me to spend more time in the garden and Nature to help my brain and body stabilise and ground itself, alongside my other treatments. And without fail it's helped.

Melissa Rae, a participant in my online survey, raised an interesting idea: 'I am going through menopause and have an all consuming urge to grow vegetables, have bare feet in my garden and my hands in the soil. I have also become an obsessed composter. I wonder if this happens to other women?'

I certainly hope so! I don't know if it's instinctive, but in my experience, gardening (and being in Nature) is definitely a way to help keep your feet on the ground, despite it shifting with massive life changes.

Gardening against the odds

Speaking of misbehaving bodies, I first met Jen Calder as a bike-riding, bushwalking, home and community-gardening uni student who was incredibly healthy, active and engaged with life. And then in 2016, out of the blue, she developed chronic fatigue syndrome (ME/CFS) and has been pretty much housebound ever since. However, she still spends some of her limited energy in her garden, which she shares with housemates. When I thought about writing this book I quickly thought about Jen – why the hell is she still gardening when she doesn't have to?

When I asked her this she replied: 'I started gardening as a student, both as a form as activism around food sovereignty, and because I was freaking out about peak oil and civilisational collapse and wanted to develop food-growing skills. Also, all the other cool activist kids were doing it. It became an identity and then a habit.'

Living with ME/CFS means that Jen can only do one main activity per day (but not every day). This interview is one of those things. 'I've been wanting to pull out my dead tomato plants for weeks but I haven't had any spare energy. I've had to learn to be happy with what I can do, and can grow, and not get upset about what I can't.'

Jen now needs a lot of help to continue gardening. Her housemate maintains the orchard and chickens, her mum helps around the garden, and Jen organises an annual working bee when it's tomato planting time: 'I provide cake and lunch, or I ask mum to cook, depending on how well I am. It's a really spirit-boosting event.'

For Jen, gardening is one of the things she risks blowing her 'energy budget' on. 'I'd have to give it a break if I got sicker again. My main motivation these days is no longer about saving the world, but simply because the food grown in my garden tastes so much better than anything I could buy. It's a very joyful and abundant thing, and connects me to the seasons, the earth and my community.'

After just under an hour we call it quits on the interview because Jen needs to rest – she's done her one thing for the day. I wrap up and go outside and pull out her dead tomato plants. Jen's disability has taken so much from her, but not her garden.

The one constant

I don't really believe in being dogmatic and 'pure' about much these days; I reckon the world is too grey and too nuanced for that. So, you'll find me eating non-organic food sometimes, and just generally being more relaxed if I don't do 'all the things' perfectly, or do them at all. But within this necessary flexibility, gardening is a permanent fixture. I drop a lot of balls in my life when I get too busy or when I'm physically unwell, but gardening has never been one of them. I reckon that means something. It's like if I dropped gardening, I'd drop a connection to a life force and groundedness that's too important to my body and spirit to compromise.

In my hardest times, where I've struggled with a body that I feel let down by, I've absolutely leant on my garden to not only physically nourish me but also to stay connected to a sense of self. I've had whole weeks of migraines where I can't really get out of bed, but I get out anyway to go stand in the garden. Just stand. Because I think, 'If I can just get out there, then that'll prove I'm going to be okay.' I'm a shit sick person – melodramatic and sad. Gardening has helped keep me strong in my spirit. When it feels like I could just float away in a puff of grey fog, gardening helps keep my feet on the ground, sometimes with just a few pea tendrils securing them, but grounded nonetheless.

For our minds

Busy, busy
brain
Interrupted
by flowers
Skipping
through
my mind

I went through a spectacularly shitty break-up as a young adult, one that I was 100 per cent responsible for initiating. Oh, the brutal irony! That season was when I also grew the plumpest, largest and most shiny crop of eggplants ever (in cool temperate Lutruwita/Tasmania this isn't an easy thing to do). Sure, these perfect eggplants were a product of a warmer than usual summer. But undoubtedly, they were also the product of me finding myself in the garden again and again – more than usual (which is a lot). I'd find myself staring at my veggie garden, not remembering how I even got there in a seemingly never-ending waterfall of disbelief, anguish and heartbreak. I nourished the eggplants' soil as I was trying to nourish myself. I breathed every type of life into it while I tried to breathe life back into my shocked and shaky heart – a seemingly impossible task and one that took much longer than a single growing season. But the garden was the most constant friend to me when I was at my most broken.

I've never grown eggplants like them since and I'm more than happy not to if it requires experiencing such scarring pain. I'm happy to settle for zucchinis in exchange for a calm and quiet heart. But from that moment on, I looked at the garden differently, with a mixture of awe and gratitude. I gave it only heartbreak and it gave me perfect eggplants.

Gardening the mind

When talking about why he gardens, author Tim Winton says that 'there's also the creaturely connection with organic reality, having your fingers in the dirt, witnessing the miracle of life happening before your eyes, day after day, week after week, month by month'.

I'm interested in what Tim calls the 'creaturely connection with organic reality'. I reckon it's this that can help us humans foster the type of mental and spiritual grounding that delivers a no-bullshit perspective and humility. Sure, gardening has given me some decent muscles and wheelbarrow-pushing oomf, but perhaps more significantly it's given my mind and my spirit enormous amounts of care.

For Bob Brown gardening is important for wellbeing:

When you go back to gardening, it connects you with the soil and it's important to us as human beings. It's not just a practical thing – there's a mystical connection there [where] we bond with this planet which (when you get rid of the cement and plastic and you get back in connection with it) elevates our wellbeing.

Many of the survey respondents expressed similar thoughts about the link between gardening and wellbeing.

- 'Accidental gardener here. Lost my mum. Found myself caring for a one-year-old, eighty-seven-year-old and chronically unwell brother. Couldn't leave the house much, so I planted some flowers to give me a sense of creativity. Soon enough the whole front yard was a cut flower garden, and after this chapter is over I now aspire to be a flower farmer. It saved me in a time of stress and grief.' **Anonymous**

- 'Because when I garden, the worries wash away and the only noise in my mind is what's in front of me. Dirt, seeds, flowers, veggies. It creates a sense of hope for the future and something to always be looking forward to too.' **Mellie Foon**

- 'I found out almost by accident that it's good for my brain, it helps me feel connected, it makes me be still in time when so much of everyday life is a blur. I couldn't stop if I wanted to.' **Anonymous**

- 'Since being diagnosed with PTSD from firefighting, I find gardening grounds me. Even if I'm having a bad day, 5 minutes in the garden can improve my outlook. And I love cooking the food I grow!' **Anonymous**

- 'I never liked gardening, everything would die. Now I'm learning as I go, and as a bonus I've found it quiets my very busy mind.' **Anonymous**

This last quote made me laugh, then it made me think how the more attention and care you give a garden the more it responds. And plant by plant, shovel by shovel, seed by seed you feel your mind go quiet, breath slow and heart pulse to the rhythm of life around you.

Grief gardening

When humans face grief or experience trauma, gardening can help. Psychologist Jill Taylor used to debrief emergency services workers and used a range of therapies to help them when they encountered challenges. She noted that, 'In a questionnaire seeking answers on which therapies helped the most, mindfulness gardening and walking in green spaces were voted as most effective.'

She had previously worked with war veterans and found that, like the emergency workers, they responded well to getting their hands in the earth. 'I found that it was helpful for people to literally get their hands in the earth (get earthed) when they were experiencing emotional difficulties,' says Taylor. 'They responded well to this and other earthing techniques and especially walking in natural green spaces.'

Gardening can be a healing hug around broken and bruised hearts. I hadn't heard of the term 'grief gardening' until I researched this book. But it is what it sounds like: people garden (or spend time in gardens) to process their grief.

- '[I] did a lot of grief gardening after Mum died. We gardened together. It connects me to her. It helps me process death when I can create life in the garden.' **Michelle Lee**
- 'I garden to bury my troubles in the dirt, to soothe the soul. It's helped with grief and PTSD. I especially love being with trees.' **Kim Cragg**
- 'I threw myself into it subconsciously after many years of dabbling as a way to process the grief of losing my brother to suicide. It became my everything – carrying me through

years of my own mental health issues and more. It gives
me a place where I feel like I truly belong when I feel
like I don't fit in anywhere else. It is how I process all my
emotions and thoughts and it has allowed me to connect
with my family and community.' **Dani G**

- 'Recently bereaved, I struggle to process my mother's death.
  Desperately wishing she was here with me, I find solace in
  the slow practice of tending to her garden. Where she once
  stood, harvesting rosellas for homemade jam that still sits
  in the fridge, I tend to snow peas and marigolds. She is the
  garden.' **Siân Chadfield**

- 'I knew, when I cared about my garden again, when I could
  think about looking after a plant, wanting a particular plant,
  that I was no longer in any danger of suicide. The garden
  was, I see now, a kind of barometer of my grief, and of
  my mental health. It was the first thing to bring me to the
  surface again and it continues to keep me afloat.' **Jordan J**

- 'Gardening connects me with the earth and my dad who
  passed away. He loved experimenting and growing native
  plants. I am growing a small patch of vegetables under the
  gumtree my dad grew from a sapling.' **Elly H**

- 'To connect with nature, mindfulness, connection with my
  dad who passed away when I was nineteen. He was an avid
  gardener and I feel him with me when I'm out in nature
  and in my garden.' **Catherine**

I think a lot of us do grief gardening without realising it.
When my mum died from the fuckery that is motor neurone disease
I was very, very sad. But I also had a type of pragmatic acceptance. You
see, Mum had embraced and merged Buddhism with her Catholic

upbringing and used to say to me, 'Hannah, make sure you imagine the people you love most dying – you need to know how to let go.'

So, from a young age I'd imagine her dying. It sounds kind of awful, and I do have memories of crying into my bedroom mirror by myself practising for when my parents would die. As a parent now that scene horrifies me but it absolutely helped me process my mum's death because I had a sense that death was coming. I knew that death was natural and that, while devastating, it's something that sits alongside life. I still do as Mum suggested, imagining the deaths of my loved ones. The only person I can't do it with is my daughter. She's simply too sacred.

But guess what? Despite having an introduction to practising Buddhist stoicism, I still felt devastatingly empty when Mum died. And while gardening wasn't something I turned to consciously, it was absolutely what I ended up doing. I liked the feeling of having a role to play. Perhaps I also liked the sense of control – something I had none of when it came to Mum dying – and the wonder of life and creativity it instilled in me. It helped me recalibrate myself on a planet that no longer had my mum balancing it out.

When I talked with Clare Bowditch she shared memories of seeing her mum in the depths of grief lying under a tree in their backyard:

I have really strong memories of my mum when I was child when she was grieving my sister's death and trying to make sense of all that, which is really hard to do obviously. And she would go and lie under this old elm tree and just lie there – and I find myself doing that for her as well.

And I remember the day it started to die, one of the boughs snapped and it was clear that it was hollowed out in the middle and I remember her having a tree specialist, an arborist come over and try and save this tree, and in the end having to accept that this tree was going … The emotional aspects and that cycle of life reminder that we get from having plants around us – it's something else.

Nature shows us clearly, relentlessly, the cycle of life and death. An ever-moving motion that you can deny and resist or accept and get in flow with. As Costa put it:

I think the garden has life and death playing out in it all the time. When we have that in our life I think it makes us more grounded. And when kids have life and death they become much more gritty, they have more capacity and it comes through having pet chickens, any animals or any plants that live or die and explain what that means and building their capacity to bounce with the flow and to move with the bumps and bruises. So I feel like the garden is such a great place to confront life head on.

A garden escape

Renowned journalist Laura Tingle was a delight to yarn with about gardening. When I spoke with her she was the ABC's chief political correspondent and at the time of writing has moved on to being the global affairs editor. It's fair to say that she doesn't exactly have much time to twiddle her thumbs, and yet she still makes time to use those thumbs to garden. When I called her it was after a particularly massive week of politics and scrutiny. I fully expected her to cancel our comparatively not-very-important garden chat. But she picked up the phone and said, 'Oh hang on, Hannah, I'm just gagging for a cup of tea.' I waited while I heard her making herself a cuppa and then we settled in for our chat. After some small talk on the week of politics that had just been, she said, 'Now let's talk about gardens, it's much more lovely.' Talk about relatable!

Like so many of us, gardening was an inherited activity for Laura:

My mother was always a great gardener when I was little. My first garden was when I was about nine years old. It was a bit accidental. A couple of plants had come up outside the fence, outside our house and I was just fiddling around one day and started to make a border and put more plants in.

It was really something with my mum. We lived in an old Federation house on this block of land in Sydney when I was little and then we moved to a place which was a very rocky, more classical 70s, more native garden. And I wasn't incredibly diligent I have to say – she did most of the work. But there were bits of garden which were mine and we spent lots of happy times going to the nursery to find new varieties of native plants and things like that.

When I asked why she bothered making the time to garden in among her very full life, Laura talked about how gardening can focus a busy mind:

In your darkest moments, it's so absorbing. Invariably you go out there and go 'I'll just do this job.' And then you go, 'Oh actually I'll just do this other job.' You're drawn into all this stuff that's happening around you all the time while you're not even watching and you're having a bit of a chat with the plants saying 'Look, just back off and give this other one a bit of a chance' – or 'C'mon, you can do better than that'. And you're problem solving – 'Why isn't this doing well, what should I plant instead?', all those things. They're such markers of time, not just the seasons. That thing where you look around and something that was really small has suddenly gotten really big. I just think it's therapeutic.

Gardens can take us out of ourselves, away from our troubles, and bring us back to ourselves at the same time, sometimes with our troubles slightly more resolved. They can create an open space where our worries, traumas, distractions and grief are gently and calmly composted back into the great universal garden that is life. They don't necessarily leave us, but they can transform. Just as food scraps can either turn into putrid anaerobic methane-emitting gunk or nutrient-dense, life-giving compost, so too can our grievances, hurts, burdens and heartbreaks transform from burning wounds into life-enhancing wonder. The type of wonder where your skin stays thin (in a good way) so that despite the exhaustion of life and death, you can still let all the love in.

Before I had fully committed to writing this book, I spiralled into the dark and boring hole that is self-doubt. I bloody hate that hole but find myself there now and then. The ongoing voice I have in my brain is that I'm worthless and nothing I do could possibly be of use to the world, so don't even bother. I was on the verge of canning the whole thing – but over the years I've practised listening to another voice that has always been there. It's little Hannah who was born with complete confidence in herself and her capacity to fully turn up and have a crack. Little Hannah is dead cool; she says things like, *You've got this mate, it's all in you.* She also says, *Get your shit together, life is not for wasting on empty thoughts like this — get over yourself and get on with it.* I bloody love her.

In the midst of this spiralling, I had a dream that I was in my thriving garden. In fact I was an actual tree with my roots deep in the ground with small native birds flying around and through me. It felt amazing. In the dream I leaned way back, dangerously so, like I might fall over, but I had to in order to admire all the bird and plant life. I remember this strong feeling that even though I was leaning outside my balance zone, there was no way I could fall over as the earth was holding me up — she had me, completely and totally. Then I woke up and got my shit together, got over myself and got on with it. Because I know that even if I do fall, the ultimate garden — our earth — will catch me and remind me that as long as I'm trying to do good and not being a dickhead then I'm doing alright. So, I wrote the book.

Because while life is inevitably hard, there are also moments of gold waiting for us. Being in my garden — digging something, planting something, mulching something, lying on the ground and breathing in the earth and patting goats — reminds me that I am the least and most interesting thing in this ecosystem of life we live in. My head and heart are better off with this knowledge.

To build community

People
together
Carrying the
load, healing
hearts
Sigh with
gratitude

I've always included flowers in my gardens, but usually with the functional lens of attracting beneficial insects, and just the ones that are edible and incredibly hardy – think calendula, heartsease, nasturtiums and borage which pop up like beautiful weeds. But in my late thirties, I started planting more flowers just because I felt like it.

One year, after a request from my daughter, I grew a single dahlia and my heart lit up. My friend Nadia Danti noticed my glee in this one dahlia plant (I wouldn't shut up about it) and came up with an idea. She was like, 'Hey Hannah, do you want to grow heaps of flowers in our backyards and give them away for free to folks in our local community doing good work as a way of saying thanks?' And so the Flower Power Project was born.

We put a call out to folks online for donations of dahlia tubers (as they get pretty expensive) and were overwhelmed with donations. I'd come home and find boxes of tubers left on my doorstep with labels such as 'pink pompon dahlias' and 'mixed box of colours' or 'forgot to label them, sorry'. That next season, we planted out whatever spare space we had across three urban-sized gardens. I planted sixty dahlia tubers in mine along with plenty of zinnias, cosmos, poppies and cornflowers.

Each Friday we'd pick bunches of flowers. People would've already nominated folks in our immediate geographic community, messaged us their love letters of appreciation and we'd then leave flowers on the nominees' doorsteps or at their workplaces. It was all love and delight.

Over that season we grew thousands of flowers, delivered many dozen bouquets and love letters and I learned a lot about growing ornamentals (something I never thought I'd 'waste my time on'). But flowers are joy on a stick! And if I'm certain of one thing in this hopefully long life, it's that among the absolute horror that humanity can be, we need more joy, more love, more joy and more love. Flowers have always been a conduit for love.

I remember when I was a kid Mum asked me what I wanted for my birthday and I said 'A bouquet of flowers *from the shop*.' She bought me a tiny bouquet and I kept it in a vase beside my bed for months and months. Even when it had turned brown and crispy I cherished it. I was just so stoked that someone cared enough for me to buy me a bunch of flowers. I felt deeply loved.

The next year we bought the Flower Power Project back in a slightly different format. Instead of delivering bouquets all over the city, we would set up a flower stall on the footpath outside the local playground. We never knew who'd walk past so it was always fun and surprising. One time, two young kids who lived across the road came over and got a bunch of flowers for their mum. Half an hour later, the mum came over with a pot of fresh tea and floral cups for us to say thanks. We'd have such broad conversations with people – about gardening (of course), but also about where people grew up, what they were studying, when their baby was due or how they loved doing craft. I'd always come home from those pop-ups with a spring in my step, with a feeling that I belonged to something really special. A community.

Some might say projects like the Flower Power Project are soft, fluffy things that don't amount to much. I'd push back on that and say community-minded projects like this are what keep our hearts pointed in the right direction. They remind us how good we can be and that reminding can maybe, just maybe, spur people into action to do good in their own communities. Acknowledging and celebrating community is how we ensure that community thrives, and in a world that's increasingly disconnected and polarised, this is something we need more of – flowers and all!

When I called Jane Edmanson to have a yarn about why she gardens, the first thing I had to do was apologise. I was running late after a hectic school drop-off.

'It's alright,' she said, 'I've been having a nice time looking through photos.'

She had come across some old black and white photos from when she first went to China in 1973 with the Australian Chinese Friendship Society – visiting shortly after former Australian prime minister Gough Whitlam had, at the tail end of the cultural revolution.

'I've always had a love of China, and Shanghai in particular. I've been there around eight times. It's amazing – you just can't believe what's happened in those two generations.'

During the short time I've known her, I've discovered that this story is 'very Jane'. She's such an unassuming person. Not only does she have incredible plant knowledge, she also surprises you with the best stories, blunt statements and, to my delight, occasional 'bad language'. When I first met this queen of ABC TV's *Gardening Australia*, I was all nerves and politeness, but she put me at quick ease with quality chat and kind eyes. She's been on national TV with *Gardening Australia* since it started in 1990 and is an ongoing, inspirational legend.

'I enjoy [gardening]. It's amazing … even looking at these funny photos from China way back in 1973. I was really shy – I was a teacher then. I was quite shy and then suddenly you get an opportunity to stand in front of a television camera and battle your way through … It's pretty amazing where life takes you. And, Hannah, your life is just starting out and you're going to do it so well, I'm really excited.'

(See what she did there? She uses her story to lift other people up – that's also 'very Jane'.)

Jane Edmanson is a big fan of community gardens:

I think community gardens are so important. People might have moved out of large gardens and come into smaller spaces but they still want to have a garden. And if they can't have a garden in their own little patch they go into a community garden and that connects people. That's such a great thing. Gardening club people – I've done a lot of talking to gardening clubs. And I've loved it. Because they're the ones that have such knowledge and they share their knowledge. I just love the way they connect with everyone and they still do! You know everywhere you go you see this lovely engagement of people and I worry that people … are engaged only with their telephone or their iPad and you think, *Put 'em down and get outside and see what's happening out there.*

Like Jane, many of my survey respondents said that they garden for the love of connection, engagement and a sense of community.

- 'I garden at a community garden and also a few hours a week in someone else's garden. It's a chance for me to engage my body and my senses and helps connect me to my community. I also feel like I've developed a different profound relationship to my produce that I've helped to cultivate.' **AM Jayatilake**
- 'It keeps me connected to something bigger than my own daily concerns. Beauty, observation of cycles and learning continues forever. Friendships and community.' **Josie C**
- 'I garden because there are so many hot women in the garden community, whoooo!!!' **Joshua S**
- 'I love being in the garden and growing food that tastes amazing that I can give to friends and neighbours and store for the year.' **Robyn Thomas**

The community garden

One of my all-time favourite community gardens is tucked away in southeast Lutruwita/Tasmania in coastal Dodges Fairy. It's called Okines Community Garden. Started by Clare Boost and Gabe Gartrell in 2002 with support from the neighbouring community house, the garden was originally a small cluster of veggie beds and fruit trees. Over the years it's grown in every possible way. While Clare and Gabe have moved on to other wonderful things, various community members have poured their talents into it to create a pumping community hub. The community garden has expanded and matured and now includes a composting toilet and an outdoor kitchen for workshops, school classes, garden programs and pizza oven events. A food cooperative was established to provide this regional town with a wholefoods shopping option. A shipping container was converted into an office for the garden coordinator and another shed popped up as a bike kitchen (fixing old bikes and making them available to people who need them).

There are no fences, and everyone is welcome to tend to the garden and harvest what they need. Back in the early days there was some mild vandalism, but one of the older women in the community camped over in the outdoor kitchen for a night here and there and had a chat with the energetic teenagers who turned up in the middle of the night. Through a number of calm chats with them the vandalism problem went away and the space is respected by everyone.

Building community means working together with all sorts of people and this region is doing that so beautifully. What started with an edible garden has brought so many different community members and groups together. It's contributed to evolving the cultural landscape of the town, attracting more people to the region. Even I consider moving out there sometimes!

These types of gardens exist all over the country and world. Just by existing they push back on the culture of individualism that dominates and shapes modern Western culture. It's a culture that says, 'Look out for yourself, be wary of one another and centre your own personal desires over the collective good.' Individualism isn't all bad, of course, but put capitalism and a marketing machine behind it that convinces people they're entitled to pretty much anything (as long as they can pay for it) and things start to get a bit iffy. This culture can put imaginary blinkers on us, guiding us to focus on only ourselves, our wants and how we can get ahead at all costs. Ultimately, it can drive us apart, and we end up isolated and alone.

But when we step into a healthy community garden, we're stepping into a different way of thinking (and being). We're stepping into the collective, where decisions aim to benefit all people involved. We're accessing and utilising public land creatively and productively, we're working together to manage the space, we're sharing skills, tools and produce, we're problem solving, making friends and learning how to communicate respectfully with people who might not think like we do. We're thinking beyond our fence lines and beyond ourselves. And that's why, when I look at these community ventures, I see only wild, beautiful rebellion against business as usual. Sure, we're growing food but we're also growing community.

When I lived in Naarm/Melbourne I was lucky enough to work with Cultivating Community, an urban agriculture enterprise that manages community and school gardens and runs community composting and food security programs. I was part of the team that helped manage community compost programs and the community gardens on housing estates across the city. These estates are huge high-rises with up to 3000 people living in each one. Many are refugees with English as a second, or fifth, language. Only a tiny fraction of residents get to have a plot at the community garden, but those who do max them out with all sorts of diverse crops. One of the gardens had a strong Asian community of gardeners who had gradually covered the whole garden in vertical frameworks for their winter melons and snake beans to grow on. Unfortunately, the state government (which owns the land) didn't like this approach to gardening and ordered the vertical frameworks be removed to improve access. The garden never really felt the same after that. It's been years since I've been back, but I like to think that the vertical structures have crept back in over time and that they're swamped with edible vines again.

In another garden it was all about eggplants for one woman from Hungary, and incredibly bitter and strong herbs that tasted like fish for some folk from China. I always wondered if growing some of their cultural foods helped soothe any homesickness they might have had or weaved some familiarity into their new world. Or maybe they just preferred their cultural foods. But while they were growing food, in some shape or form they were also growing community – sharing moments in the garden with their neighbours, swapping seeds, cuttings and tricks on improving soil health. Every interaction looped them together with threads of connection.

Kitana Mansell is a proud Palawa woman from Lutruwita/Tasmania. She is developing a bushfood garden at Piyura Kitina/Risdon Cove, just outside of Nipaluna/Hobart. The goal of the garden is to bring native plants back into the soil and inspire young people to get out into the garden, planting and playing around with bush foods in schools.

Kitana is such a powerhouse. She didn't grow up with plant and gardening knowledge, which was largely destroyed with colonisation of Lutruwita/Tasmania; instead she started learning about native plants when she was seventeen years old doing her business traineeship, working alongside gardening expert Angus Stewart.

Once I started learning from Angus, the kind of scientific side of things, I'd go back to my community and start learning from others and I realised that all these foods have been eaten by my people and still some people do today. And so that's where I really started learning about these plants [and that we needed] to learn how we can regrow them and bring them back to Country.

If you know what you're looking for, you'll often see these plants cruising along coastlines and rambling through the bush. They are plants such as pigface (*Carpobrotus rossii*), saltbush (*Atriplex nummularia*), samphire (*Sarcocomia quinqueflora*), yam daisy (*Microseris lanceolata*), chocolate lily (*Fritillaria biflora*), river mint (*Mentha australis*) and Tasmanian flax lily (*Dianella Tasmanica*). They're just some of the plants that have helped sustain the oldest living culture in the world.

Eventually, Kitana plans on welcoming the broader community into this garden so they can also learn about Aboriginal foods. I'm continuously struck by the generosity so many Aboriginal and Torres Strait Islander folk exude, including Kitana. In the process of reclaiming knowledge that was ripped away from her ancestors, she open-heartedly shares so much of it with non-Aboriginal people, building community. I see Kitana's work as so blindingly important in rebuilding culture and connection to Country – gradually reclaiming it plant by plant.

Crossing divides

I've met countless gardeners and farmers, and sometimes I wonder if we're going to connect and get along. One time I was at an agricultural show in a rural region with what felt like 400 tractor stalls and lots of big hats. I walked into the marquee where I was due to give a talk on edible gardening and compost and felt lots of eyeballs land on me. There were lots of farmer types and I reckon I was the youngest by around thirty years. I couldn't help but notice that no one else had pink hair or tattoos of garden paraphernalia. I took a deep breath and smiled. Turns out that under their big hats and my pink hair we had the same love of the land and of life running through our veins. I did my talks and then stayed around as long as I could yarning with this gorgeous community. Despite our differing dress sense, we had everything important in common.

Costa expands on this.

I think out of all the hobbies and all the pursuits, gardening is one where people are some of the most caring and sharing. They share their ideas and they share their experiences, compared to other places where people are a bit more protective. But if you ask someone who's a gardener for help, I don't know — I've never had someone to tell me to get nicked! Never! Doesn't work that way. So that's kinda special in its own right.

It's so true. Despite any potential social friction between folks, once you work out that someone is a gardener, there is usually a lot to discuss, share, swap and investigate together. Any differences slide into the 'not as important as learning more about compost' basket. Gardens help us build relationships in some of the more unlikely places.

One time while in Meanjin/Brisbane I had a series of conversations about gardening with wildly different people. On Friday evening I was at an event for an art portraiture prize where I talked to all sorts of people including a couple who were introduced to me as being 'big supporters of the arts' (I think this is code for being rich). I nervously glanced at the woman's pearls and wondered what I could talk with them about. But once we worked out that we had gardening in common we quickly talked deeply about how we both garden with the focus of creating good lives and landscapes – using gardening and landscape management as a tool to do good for the hope and health of the future.

The night after the fancy art event I sat around a mate's dinner table and listened to new friend Matty wax lyrical about his love for managing the Neighbourhood Farm. Matty is a curly haired, booming-voiced, sparkly eyed, big-hearted softy with two very big green thumbs. The farm he runs is a 1500 square metre urban farm bordering Oxley and Corinda in Meanjin/Brisbane. From this space Matty feeds thirty-five households and seven cafes each week with fresh organic produce.

On the face of it, you wouldn't expect to find many commonalities between Matty, myself and the arty couple. But, after shaking off my subconscious judgemental side, I found many common threads weaving us together, forming connections the soil food web would be proud of.

Bruce Pascoe believes that gardening can be key to learning to love your country and the people in it: 'I always remember [former Australian Liberal politician] Jeff Kennett declaring that he was a great

gardener. That completely softened my impression of Kennett …
we're miles apart politically and emotionally probably. But I thought –
he likes his garden, he's not all bad. We've got to find the humanity in
each other and respect it.'

This last sentence lives rent free in my brain. Our world is
increasingly polarised, with an invisible, sometimes quiet, sometimes
loud cultural pressure to pick a side. But what happens if we refuse
to? What happens if we hang in the thick of nuance with the many
complexities of humanity? What if we engage in critical and deep
thinking to find the intersections with issues and people that are
almost always there? Of course it's quicker, cleaner and easier in the
short term to just pick a side. But in the long term it hurts us by
pulling us further and further apart. The more we can find connection
between one another, the closer we come to peace, both internally
and externally. As Bruce mentioned, this doesn't mean you are
suddenly politically or emotionally aligned, but it does mean that
you're able to recognise some common good in one another.

I thought I'd put this to the test by reaching out to some former
and current politicians who I'm mostly not politically aligned with
(and who I suspected I didn't have much or anything in common
with). I sent out numerous emails to politicians of different stripes, and
got either crickets or polite rejections. The only political person who
responded was former Greens leader Bob Brown.

So, my test didn't amount to much, but when I thought about it,
I am constantly seeking the commonalities in people. I meet all sorts
of folks in my line of work and I love it. One time I was sitting in
an audience waiting to get up to be a keynote speaker at a gardening
gathering. I got talking to the elderly couple next to me and had
a delightful yarn with them about our shared love of gardening.
When the conference organisers got our attention and did an official

acknowledgement of Country and of all Aboriginal and Torres Strait Islander peoples, the woman whispered 'Oh, not this again' and started tut tut tutting through the whole acknowledgement. Immediately, I could see that while our love of gardens was on common ground, our politics was on different planets. I then got up and did the keynote talk for the conference and made sure to weave in how magnificent it is that people's shared love of gardens can bridge the gap between them regardless of their backgrounds, culture or politics. Afterwards I sat down next to the couple and they generously showered me with praise for my talk. Did I raise the differences we had in our politics? No, in that particular setting I chose to raise our similarities instead in the hope that we can strengthen and grow together and not apart.

I also put this to the test all the time in my daily life, with my dad in particular. We have a lot of political views in common except I'd say he's more conservative and stuck in his ways and he'd say I'm more idealistic. And we really piss each other off sometimes because we're both stubbornly convinced we're right. But when we're talking about gardening, or when we're in a garden, it's all 'Oooo, ahhhh and look at the bird and what do you think about this plant and where should I put a frog pond and this is so beautiful, let's go pat the goats.'

Our shared obsession with gardens has also helped me process baggage I've had with my dad that I've been carrying since childhood. And since my dad moved to Lutruwita/Tasmania to be closer to some of us kids, things have shifted for me in our relationship. We haven't hung out this much since I was a child. One day I felt the heavy weight of a younger, sad Hannah lift off me. She just stood up and walked away. Actually she skipped away! She skipped down a garden path towards the macadamia tree where one of our inexpertly built tree houses was and she was wearing a cotton purple tartan dress with sparkly flecks (my favourite dress when I was in kindergarten).

Gardens can heal and a shared love of gardens can build incredible connections between vastly different people. Just as Bruce said, 'We just have to find the humanity in each other and respect it.' No doubt about it, when we cultivate the land there's enormous potential to cultivate rich and meaningful connections with both the place and the people nearby.

How one community grew from a garden

My mates Brenna and Charlie who live in Denmark, south-west Western Australia, describe themselves as big community people. When visiting them I immersed myself in their community as much as I could. On Tuesday evening we went to the local soup night (Soupy), Wednesday evening was life drawing class, Thursday evening was choir and Friday morning was dance class. It was the best. But one of the most powerful ways they've become part of, and built, community is through food and gardens, starting with their local food cooperative. Brenna explains: 'It means you get to meet other people you wouldn't necessarily get to meet. Like giving away tomato seedlings … the outcome of that was for me to be able to say hi to lots of lovely people. And encourage trade and encourage connections.'

When Brenna had surplus tomato seedlings she could have simply offered the seedlings for free, but instead she invited people to participate in 'the great tomato trade'. It turned into a wonderful event of food and connection.

We got the best fresh bread from the oven sourdough (artisan style) that lasted 2.5 seconds here. We got bunches of flowers, homemade herbal tea mix which was delightful, dozens of eggs from three different people, loads of different vegetables. Someone gave me bunches of parsley, and I already had my own parsley but I didn't have *their parsley* so I was stoked. It was just the surprise of it every day and being able to meet people. And now they're coming to grab other things from us, like books[47] or veggies and I'm getting to see them again and again.

I put it to Brenna and Charlie that from the outside looking in, it seems that food is almost like a currency of goodwill in the community. 'Yeah,' replies Charlie. 'It's like a type of currency, but the beautiful thing about it is that it's not a transactional currency – it's a circular currency.'

This speaks to keeping currency (in all its forms) mostly within the geographical community for its own benefit. In particular, Charlie talks about the gift economy where people don't barter; rather they gift things to one another with no expectation of having that being repaid. They trust that the community will hold one another through times of abundance or scarcity. That when they might be in need people will support them.

In the name of cultivating abundance one of their friends [Olly] made up a game of sorts based on winning.

> Brenna: 'If he invites us to dinner to his place three times and we haven't reciprocated it's not that we're in debt, it's that we're in sort of friendly one-upmanship where he's winning. So we've gotta lift our game.

> Charlie: 'So the person who gives the most, wins.'

Brenna: 'So we can be happy for him that he's winning that part of it but I've given him way more carrots because I know his children are obsessed – so I'm winning on that level. We're all winning!'

Now that's a game I can embrace! See how much you can care for your community and strengthen and grow it in the process. And also win – my competitive spirit loves this idea.

Walking and riding our bikes around Denmark over the week I saw lots of edible gardens sprawling through front yards and spilling over onto the verge. It's the kind of place where wildlife is not devouring edible plants, so there's very little or no fencing at all (the opposite of southern Lutruwita/Tasmania where I live). And this actually helps create more catalysts for community connection.

When Brenna noticed two beautiful mulberry trees down the bottom of the hill across from each other she decided to reach out to the people who lived there. 'I wrote them each a letter and gave them my number and said please contact me as I'd like to harvest them and I'll give you some jam at the end,' says Brenna. Both people wrote back to enthusiastically give Brenna their blessing to harvest the fruit. 'What I didn't expect from that exchange,' says Brenna, 'is that it's deepening my connection to [this] place and to this ecology … I have a story with that tree now … It's almost like I put a root down in that soil – it's like a song line in the modern sense, that it's [the process of becoming] part of this ecosystem.'

Brenna and Charlie see an opportunity to connect pretty much everywhere. Combined with their talents and hard work, they're constantly looking for the next thing they can do to build community through their work and life – something that permaculture has deeply informed due to its focus on cultivating connections with everything and everyone. When it comes to community, Charlie says it beautifully in that we're 'gardening people instead of plants'.

On my last full day visiting, we met one of their friends, Rhian, who showed us around the bus she was retrofitting into a tiny home. Rhian's a talented musician and taught the choir class we went to earlier in the week. Brenna and I were telling her about that morning's dance class and she asked us to show her. So we pumped the tunes, took off our shoes and went out to the little paddock surrounded by forest and did our contemporary dance we'd learned that morning. As I was leaping through the grass, whirling my arms and head around, laughing with the sun on my face I felt free and content. I realised that the only reason I was there, dancing in this paddock feeling so happy, was because of gardening. It was gardening that brought Brenna, Charlie and I together as peers, then friends – and I'm so grateful.

Gardening has shaped my life in so many ways, including helping me to find my people, my community, so that we can dance and leap through life together.

To connect with Nature

Dreaming
of flying
Through
forests,
over oceans
I am the
sunrise

While I happily live in cool temperate Lutruwita/Tasmania, each time I visit subtropical Meanjin/Brisbane where I grew up, my whole body breathes out with a sensation of 'Oh, there you are.' It's the verdant plants, the humid air, the squawking birds, the golden light and the hum of home in my blood. My connection to that place is forever and a piece of me only comes to life when I'm there.

But there are other pieces of me that are now planted in my home garden in Nipaluna/Hobart. With every passing season I live here, my relationship to this place grows — like a gnarly taproot it just keeps on growing deeper and deeper. We have our ups and downs, but mostly we just grow more and more entwined. While the sparkling air and the lush green of the subtropics helped grow me up, it's the silver light of Lutruwita/Tasmania that will probably see my hair go silver with it (if I ever stop dying it pink, that is). I wasn't born here, but I think I'll probably die here and that's a happy thought.

Many of my connections with the land, with Nature, are through my garden and that is one of the reasons I'm happily obsessed with gardening my little patch.

Connection to Country

I've long listened to Aboriginal and Torres Strait Islander peoples talk about the importance of having connection to Country. How the concept of Country is not restricted to only physical land, how Country is also a 'deeply symbolic and spiritual place'. Having a strong connection to Country means you have a strong connection to yourself, your culture and your people.[48]

When Australia was colonised in 1788, control over land and waterways and any sense of ownership was gradually taken from all Aboriginal and Torres Strait Islander Peoples. This dispossession ultimately compromised their connection to Country, their identity and sense of belonging in their own home.

When I spoke to Bob Brown he reflected on the connection to Country:

> [Today] Aboriginal people around the country have the poorest health and disease and there's many more of them in jail and it's just wrong. Because their land and culture was stolen – *when you give back land you give back culture* as well and that gives people spirit and strength and a sense of being on this planet and what's more we have a lot to learn from them in terms of the importance of Country.

I asked Palawa woman Kitana Mansell whether non-Aboriginal

people can have their own version of connection to Country:

> Yeah, I think [non-Aboriginal people] can have a connection to
> Country for sure – and I do see a lot of people just connecting.
> But I think the only way you can really connect is learning the
> true history of the place and working with Aboriginal people
> and really supporting and working with them.
>
> I guess if you live in your own kind of bubble and you're
> not really learning about this soil that's underneath where you
> live and understand the rich history of the place. I feel like once
> non-Aboriginal people dive into that more then they will start
> to feel that sense of connection and feel how lucky they are to
> be living on this land.

I feel so much truth in what Kitana says. The sense of connection
I have with the patch of Muwinina land I live on in Nipaluna/Hobart
deepens the more I reflect on how I stand and garden on the very
broad shoulders of Palawa Aboriginal people. I've always believed that
we have nothing to lose and everything to gain when we open our
hearts and minds to the history of modern Australia and learn about
the oldest living culture in the world – Aboriginal and Torres Strait
Islander culture.

Bruce Pascoe also believes that non-Aboriginal people can have a
connection to land: 'They have to. You ask so many older Aboriginal
people, it's not a universal sentiment amongst mob, but a lot of people
will say that we can't afford to have non-Aboriginal people not
loving their country.' Bruce goes on to say that there are 'two facts
of Australian history: black fellas aren't going to go away and white
fellas aren't going to go away ... We have to make sure we allow and
encourage non-Aboriginal to love this country. If not, they'll just be

wilful destructive spirits. And we're seeing that now. We're seeing how people have lost contact with their country.'

Bruce goes on to say that when it comes to Aboriginal and non-Aboriginal people 'we can work together ... whether it's language or environmental stories. Old Uncle Max[49] said "If I'm going to keep my culture, I have to give it away."'

Such pragmatic generosity cracks my heart a little. Aboriginal and Torres Strait Islander people I've talked with and listened to over the years have been overwhelmingly gracious in advocating for the need to work together towards a better future for all. We all win when we adopt this mentality.

Connecting to Nature, connecting to life

My gateway to caring for and connecting to the land I live on and travel through has mostly been through practical gardening and farming. This is something that I have in common with Mickey Robertson from Glenmore House in New South Wales.

> I believe it's in productive gardening that the real stimulation and understanding of connection ... to soil, land, climate and seasons becomes truly evident. Then, to garden in a productive way becomes a real need: productive gardening becomes an extension of self, suggesting and guiding a routine ... and creating a way of life ...
>
> Productive gardening truly is about health and wellbeing ... and my belief is that you will be repaid in spades for effort spent, as well as spoiled with some of the most beautiful visual delights, let alone tastes ... on earth. What more could one need

to motivate? Aside from sharing it!

I'm convinced that each and every gardener has their own special way of connecting with Nature through their garden. Let me share a less common way I connected with Nature while living in share houses … I made composting toilets in wheelie bins. I got the design from a company called Natural Event which uses the wheelie loos for music festivals. Not only were they a great design for a compost loo, they were dead easy to move house with. I'd borrow a ute, wheel my composting loo onto the back of it, drive it across town to its new home, park it in the shed and carry on. I felt like this was smart behaviour. And I still do! Turning my shit into gorgeous compost that would eventually (after twelve months of worm farm composting) return to perennial gardens. There was no way I was leaving my humanure behind. People would be like, 'What on earth are you doing?' and I'd be like, 'Mate, I'm basically *making* earth like a poo magician.'

One of Anton's old friends had another slightly offbeat way of connecting with Nature. '[They] got into gardening from growing marijuana (*Cannabis sativa*), that was their entry to gardening,' Anton tells me. 'They got really good at soil health and plant care. Lots of people who turned into very good gardeners got their green thumb from growing weed. One of them got so good that they ended up running a commercial food farm (not growing weed) for over a decade.'

I take great delight in the many entry points to gardening. Sure, some of them might be illegal in parts of the world. But we all end up at the same place – tending our carrots, caressing roses and whispering to our soil. Being in relationship with Nature.

Convenience versus Nature

Evan Williams, the co-founder of online social platform Twitter, now known as X, once stated in a *New York Times* interview: 'Convenience seems to make our decisions for us, trumping what we like to imagine are our true preferences. (I prefer to brew my coffee, but Starbucks instant is so convenient I hardly ever do what I 'prefer.') Easy is better, easiest is best.'[50]

I love convenience and seek it out often, although sometimes hesitantly. I was around thirty-eight the first time I lived with a dishwasher, and I was amazed by how good it was. For a long time, I was philosophically opposed to having 'another thing' in the house: another thing to spend money on, another thing to fix when it breaks, another thing to clean. But my mother-in-law gently insisted on buying us one (thanks Ros) and we were smitten. This quietly humming magic machine gave us time – the most priceless gift of all. Each day we save between 30 and sixty minutes, so between 180–335 hours per year. That's real, solid time right there. There was a twelve-month period when friends would ask how we were doing and we'd just talk about how good the dishwasher was. It was life changing!

But I'm also a fan of a bit of inconvenience. I reckon it keeps us grounded to reality, to what really matters.

Years ago I attended a leadership course and spoke with another participant about agriculture and food systems. This person said something along the lines of, 'Wouldn't it be better, more convenient, if we could just buy eggs in powder form in a packet? That would be great progress.'

Firstly, I checked and you can buy this product already. Secondly, I disagreed. Why? I'm not fundamentally against powdered eggs and, depending on which version you buy, some appear to be nutritionally good. But I think when we actively and consistently choose to turn recognisable food items (i.e. an egg) into non-recognisable food items (i.e. egg powder), we're breeding a type of disconnect from Nature. We're putting more distance between us and our ability to 'read' Nature, to recognise her in her original form.

I happen to believe that disconnection is the root rot we face in this world. When you're disconnected from someone or something it's easier to make decisions that impact it negatively – decisions that degrade it, take away from it, log it, mine it, bomb it, kill it, pollute it or harm it in some way.

But when you have a connection with something or someone, there's a thread of care looping you together. When I see a chicken's egg, I think of the chicken. I think of its home, its nesting box and the outside areas it scratches through searching for bugs and slugs. I wonder what type of breed the chook is, what colour her feathers are. When I look at egg powder, I think of shiny plastic packets on supermarket shelves, protein inputs and gym bros.

Imagine if all our food came as types of powders, wrapped in shiny packets for convenience? The hiker and camper in me who spends hours dehydrating food into lightweight crumbs and powders would love this (and absolutely buys some of this). But not as an everyday thing! Heavily processing foods fundamentally shifts how we relate to it and impacts our knowledge and connection to Nature. The more connections we can find and foster the better, so no – I don't think we should replace eggs with powdered eggs. I think we should embrace a touch of inconvenience, where possible, if it means strengthening our connection to Nature.

'Back paddock' spirituality

Edible gardening was my first teacher that helped me understand the interconnectedness of us all. I don't know if I have what you could call a spiritual connection to land, but there's something there. I remember having a chat with my dad as a young kid. While Mum would go to St Mary's church in West End most weeks[51] Dad would go out to 'the back paddock' – a corner of the herb nursery next to the orange trees and beneath the large gum trees where you couldn't see any houses. Each day he'd be down there with a cup of instant coffee in the morning and a beer in the evening. I remember asking him why he didn't go to church with Mum and he said, 'This is my church, out here in the back paddock.' I asked him about this again while I was writing this book and he said:

> Sitting in the back garden, watching the sun coming down through the plants ... I remember a golden nasturtium in the evening sunlight, it glowed and the breeze moved it. It was a combination of the plant, with the sun and the air movement and the result of nutrients through the soil, the stems into one flower. And I remember thinking, 'That is creation.'

He also showed me some writing he did about that time about that back paddock spot in particular: 'At dawn before breakfast and work and afterwards in the evening, I made a habit of sitting quiet in this Creation, as I referred to it, and I would find my inner self and wonder at the way in which life can resurrect.'

I remember joining him on some of those evenings, looking up at the dusk sky, listening to the chortling birds in the gums and smelling the warmth of the earth being released from the day and thinking

'Yeah, that makes sense to me.' There's some type of invisible spiritual connection there for me – it's shaped like a lemon-scented gum, smells like warm earth and feels like soil under my toes.

Making time for reverence

While gardening has been my gateway to connect with land and Nature, bushwalking and camping have been the catalyst for my deeper understanding that *we are Nature*. When you're 'out there' it's the ultimate experience of *just being* in landscape and letting the magic of it all move through you.

During late August and early September 2024 I walked through the Larapinta Trail in the Northern Territory with eight friends. We covered 230 kilometres slowly over seventeen days and every step felt like meeting a new friend in the arid landscape. A mixture of delightful surprise, curiosity and grateful wonder that we even got to be immersed in such powerful company.

It was unseasonably hot with temperatures soaring to 40 degrees in late winter (we were told to expect mid 20s at the most and cool frosty nights, so you could say we were a little caught off guard). The temperatures were so high I ended up ditching my tent and sleeping on a $4 tarpaulin, and borrowed a mozzie net from a local (thanks Katie). For the whole walk I was soaked in a combination of sweat and awe in equal measure. One day one of our mates was so hot she walked half naked from around 4am until sunrise 'with her girls out' (her boobs) because it was simply too hot to put a shirt on. For the first few days a couple of us had different versions of blood noses. In hindsight we probably had mild heat stroke for that first bit while our cool temperate bodies adjusted to the shocking summer-level heat of arid Australia. But no complaints – we were bloody stoked through the whole experience!

We struck gold as our trip coincided with the best wildflower season in twenty years. We all melted into a giddy mess of plant enthusiasts. We had to stop every metre to admire flowers we'd never seen before. Taking photos, getting down on our hands and knees to have a sniff, pulling out the plant flip chart to ID them and making many loud declarations of delight. And the birds! Hours were spent watching them daily. Special mention to the fluorescent green budgerigars we watched going in and out of the perfect hollows in a river red gum tree at the Hugh Gorge Junction campsite. After I got home I began painting the birds that I saw on the trip. I just kept going and painted dozens of birds from all over the country and over a year later I'm still painting. It was as if spending time in the raw Larapinta landscape recalibrated my brain and heart to obsess over all the important things: birds, plants, soil, rocks, the sky, the stars, more birds! Even the giant woma python that woke me up one night 40 centimetres from my face was important.

Each day when we reached our camp for the night I'd end up lying on the earth. Shoes off, hat off, sun shirt off – just shorts and a crop top. I'd sprawl on the ground getting deeply dirty with red earth. We swam at every opportunity but otherwise I was covered in a fine layer of red earth and I felt clean. I hadn't felt so connected to myself, to Earth, to life for ages.

I thought I might do lots of writing while on the trail, but my brain went blank and it was the best. Sometimes the most productive thing we can do is nothing. Allow our brains a chance to breathe out, to settle into a new pattern. Or perhaps remember old patterns of calm that are just hiding beneath layers of busy. And then towards the end of the walk this haiku fell out of me …

I walked through landscape
And the landscape walked through me
Friends forever now

There were some important learnings for me on that trip. The first being that I simply must sleep outside more without a tent, just under the stars, even if only in my backyard.[52] I love being surrounded by the world and only the world. I think it helps me breathe better and deeper. I seem to sleep and dream better and deeper as well.

The second is that I would greatly benefit from doing more long bushwalks. It usually takes at least four days for my brain to relax on the track. After that a layer of calm descends, wrapping my brain in a warm hug. It's still busy, but the thoughts wash through me instead of getting stuck on the knobbly bits of my brain where they can have a habit of festering.

And finally, I took away the big affirmation that life is all about connection to people and place. When I first started organising the Larapinta trip I thought I'd just go by myself as it'd be easier to arrange and I quite enjoy my own company. But I put the call out to see if other mates would be keen and I'm so grateful I did. It reminded me that investing time in friendships is investing in quality of life. And I'm forever grateful to have walked through Larapinta with such good people. To have shared many big conversations, struggles, jokes and magical memories that will loop us together forever.

Like all good relationships, my version of having a connection to landscape is ever evolving. The less time I make for it the more elusive it feels. The more time I invest in it, the stronger it gets and the stronger I get. It's that simple.

When I got back to Nipaluna/Hobart, I saw my home and garden with fresh eyes. Often us gardeners have trouble seeing anything except all the jobs we have to do, but all I could see was beauty and love. Yes, I still have to pull weeds, water seedlings and mulch the orchard but I do so remembering that I'm part of the heartbeat of it all.

My friend Jen Calder expresses the connection between gardening and Nature perfectly: 'Every time I eat some kale from my garden, I could sit for a moment and be like "I watched you grow, I made the compost for you" – it's an amazing reciprocal plant/human relationship. I haven't been making time for this reverence, but I could.'

We could all make more time for reverence, for connecting with and appreciating Nature. But life is busy and sometimes just getting plants in the ground, or getting them watered while you're juggling ten other jobs, is a small miracle. What's the solution? Seeking out small moments of connection that you can then piece together to form a larger, stronger foundation for existing. Whether it's buying fresh eggs over powdered, sitting in the backyard at dusk, learning more about native plants, camping next to your veggie patch or going on a bushwalk with friends. Take the moments you can to connect with the land, with Nature, with yourself. You won't regret it.

To connect to culture and our own histories

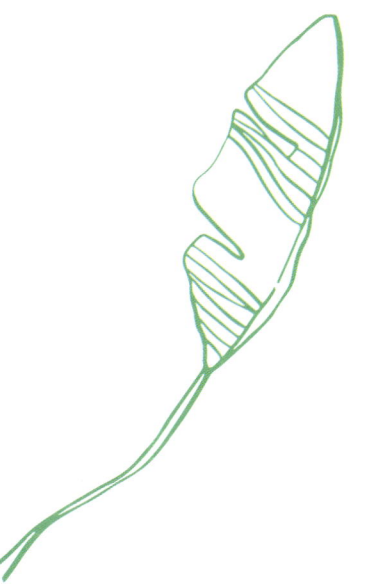

If you look
closely
You'll see fizzy
living links
Connecting
us all

Smelling a particular scent or hearing a nostalgic song has the power to transport us back in time, unlocking memories from a different period of our lives. I believe that gardens and plants have this same magical quality about them. If it's a good memory, a lot of us (consciously or not) will try to replicate the trigger so we can experience it again and again. This is one of the many reasons I garden: to help keep treasured memories close to the surface of my heart.

For me, one of my happy triggers is the unassuming seaside daisy (*Erigeron glaucus*). This is a very common, small daisy plant (the non-invasive species) that loves to grow out of rocks and cracks in the footpath. Without fail every time I see it I think of my mum, Maria, who had two beautiful brown thumbs. But she married a gardener and lived in the middle of a herb nursery so she had a crack at a few things. She took a shine to the subtropical shrubs in pots on the veranda and a couple of clusters of seaside daisy growing out of rubble on either side of the front gate. It's these hardy 'can't kill if you tried' daisies that bring her big smiling face and warm hugs to mind.

I have a memory of her standing at our green front fence watering the daisies, looking unreasonably proud of her success in growing them. Nobody told her that you don't really need to water them. They thrive on neglect, but we didn't want to tell her – we just gifted her the moment. Thanks to this memory, I've planted a few dozen seaside daisies around my garden, including near the main gate to our home. Having these plants in my garden means that I feel my mum's presence and hear her laugh multiple times each day.

Heritage gardening

Gardens connect us to our cultures and to our histories. Some of my earliest memories are in the garden. I have sensory memories where I know I'm sitting on the grass and Dad's nearby somewhere working in the herb nursery. Mum went back to work pretty quickly after having me (I was the last of five kids so good for her!), so Dad was my primary caregiver. This meant that I was plonked down in the garden a lot while he worked. The air is sticky with humidity, birds are chortling, warm sun is on my skin, there's grass between my fleshy little fingers. These are the memories that make us, that we build our whole lives on.

Costa also has core memories of a childhood garden – his grandparents' garden in Sydney.

The layers of memory in [my grandparents' garden] – from the dahlias and the sweet peas in the front yard and the carnations and the aromas. And the colours! You'd know when it was sweet pea season cause you had these water pipes with wire around them and it was just a wall across half the front yard. And then you had the carnations just along the footpath and they gave off the smell …

If I could sit with my grandparents now and talk to them about what I see and know and explain to them that my memory of them is so strong, that's it's carried for life. I [get] a little bit sort of happy/teary about that. Because making memories is the most important thing we can do in our life. And to make memories for others – the garden is such a beautiful place to do that and the memories are so sensory that you can impact someone through the colour, the smell, through the taste, through the sound of the birds and then through the touch through the chickens, or whatever it is.

I remember when I went back to Greece for the first time and I could speak Greek – it was almost like the country knew me better, not just the people – but the country. [It was special] to go back to my grandmother's island, meet some of the relatives and see her house and go down to the allotments for agriculture, to go there and walk these little laneways and know that she walked there. And then to go to this cousin's allotment and pick the beans and pick the okra and all these different things. And I remember I went for a swim and they said 'come up for lunch' and I had this lunch that captured all of the love of all those generations of the family. And I'm not talking this up. That meal was one of the tastiest. It was wholesome because it was more than just the taste. It was what had gone into the soil. It was the love that they shared that I was there and that they were connection to my grandmother and then all of that connection was going beyond them and it was like this incredibly holistic moment where the flavour of the whole exchange was the most incredible thing. And you know, it wasn't about how they made the compost. It was coming out of the minerals in the rocks and the history and it was like in a sense – hey, you're part of this – you're home and you can taste this.

Connection to people, place and culture run deep with all types of gardeners. And gardening is the perfect activity to do with family to foster connections across generations. Author Tim Winton said:

I'd like to think my grandkids will learn some basic gardening skills. For their own satisfaction and mental health, but also as a survival skill. And maybe to keep a little bit of family culture alive. I have fond memories of picking figs with my grandmother, or shelling peas with her and all these years later I've had my grandkids pick lemons, olives, grapes and tomatoes alongside me many times.

Growing, tending and harvesting food together is pretty fundamental and healthy human behaviour. In the face of so much atomised, abstract and virtual behaviour – all those families sitting around alone together in a room or a house locked into their devices, it looks positively prophylactic! You can have a conversation with someone while you're picking figs, or making pesto, or washing lettuce. Or you can feel close to them while saying nothing at all. There's no techno-feudalist algorithm robbing you and holding you captive.

Indeed there isn't; there's just Nature doing what she does best ... existing and allowing us to do so the same. Winton continues:

I think passing on some gardening skills to your kids and grandkids could have a material effect on their happiness and survival. Recently, my oldest grandson grew carrots for the first time. He was so proud. They looked a bit like my first lot — with faces only a mother would love. Woody as a 1980s chardonnay. But they were mighty.

My hope is that there will always be kids growing ugly carrots and showing them off with disproportionate pride. It's these ugly carrots that are creating memories and connection within families, shaping a shared history and knowledge that can be passed on from one gardener to the next.

Jane Edmanson grew up on a citrus farm, and her mum was one of the first people to grow old-fashioned heritage roses where she lived in Mildura, Victora. Jane remembers driving along the road and her mum screeching to a halt and saying, 'There's a rose, I'm going to go take a cutting!'

[I'd think] 'oh my god, mother — really!' But she was a great gardener, she loved her garden, she did it really well. People still say, 'Oh, we remember your mother's garden.' It was a really lovely garden and she managed to spread her love of plants to all of us and to the nieces and nephews.

I think any teenagers of fanatical gardeners know this feeling of heart-in-the-stomach embarrassment when your parent loses all social inhibitions in public to 'get that cutting' they didn't even know they *needed*. My daughter is only ten, but she's already flinging death stares my way whenever I pause to take a little cutting, or stop to talk to someone in their front garden.

I love hearing about Jane's dad as well: 'He loved growing avocadoes and lemons and oranges … He was a very kind man and he translated that to the earth. How important soil is and how farmers have to be really careful. They are the guardians of our land in a way.'

All of our parents and caregivers are guardians of the culture we grew up in – they shape our memories, which then shape who we are. I think of our own daughter. Just this morning I asked if she liked gardening. 'It's just so booooorrrring, I don't like the process of digging the earth or planting the seeds. But I do like eating the peas.' Pretty relatable, actually. Little Hannah mostly found gardening boring too – but that didn't stop me absorbing my family culture. It didn't stop me learning by osmosis and didn't stop my head and heart's curiosity being piqued.

Regardless of how our kid chooses to live her life, we know that we've planted a seed inside her, infused with care and connection of land, and also the knowledge of how to make compost. In the meantime, we make sure to plant large patches of pea crops staggered throughout the season that will happily lure her into the garden, where memories are made that help make up our family culture.

Growing culture

As a child, author Bruce Pascoe was more interested in football and cricket. But it was his mum's love of gardening (and his love of his mum) that made him pay attention to the garden.

I didn't understand as a kid, but I can see it meant so much to her ... because I love my mother and she was a person of such great depth I knew there was something there that was important and I found that I've remembered everything she said. Plants that she particularly loved – I keep on finding them in people's gardens and taking cuttings. I'm planting them now and I never thought I would. I was philosophically opposed to roses because of the British rose but I still love them [because my mother loved them].

Before Bruce's mum passed away he had a photo taken of her:

We had a beautiful photo of my grandmother just before she passed away and she had a camellia above her head. She was reaching for it and had her face next to it – a classic photograph. So when Mum was very ill, I replicated this photograph and gave it to her and for all her sisters. That was a really important photograph. Those women have gone now – two of the sisters had the two photos side by side. My cousin and I talked about it just the other night – we normally talk football but we talked about those two photographs and how important they were. I said – have you still got them? And he said yeah, they're in the living room and I've still got my two.

People and plants. Plants and people. The connections weave back and forth across generations and keep love and memories alive.

As a result of the success of his 2014 book *Dark Emu* Bruce is now growing Aboriginal foods on his Mallacoota farm as a way for 'Aboriginal people [to] be employed growing their own cultural food. So it's a cultural act as well as an economic act and it's also going to be a sovereignty act in the long run.'

The book generated so much interest in Aboriginal culture and specifically traditional foods. Bruce could see that there was a risk that traditional foods might be taken away from Aboriginal people, used by non-Aboriginal chefs keen to integrate new foods into their culinary worlds. So, he and a team of like-minded people got farming to retain autonomy and control of their traditional food and culture.

What Bruce and his team are doing is a gorgeous act of solutions-based activism towards cultural and land rights for Aboriginal people. He goes on to say that what Aboriginal and Torres Strait Islander people don't have enough of is their own land:

Aboriginal people have got to be able to take over these run-down sheep farms that are dead as door nails now and closed up houses and people have walked off them. The bank has given up. Give them to us – we'll fix them because we'll plant the plants on those bits of land that should've been there originally, so that'll be the salt bushes, the tuber that grows in that Country. Its root will be half a metre down below the surface because that's how it gets its moisture and it stays healthy. That's what we'll do.

I see Bruce's gardens as a part of restoring and evolving his and other Aboriginal people's connection to Country. By growing traditional plants and practising culture while doing so, he's breathing life back into degraded landscapes and simultaneously breathing fresh air and determination into the oldest living culture in the world. Onya Bruce!

Much of Costa's work takes him through remote Aboriginal communities across Australia. He set about learning from the people he met, educating himself about what having a connection to Country and being on Country means:

I remember when I first heard the concept of 'being on Country' and I didn't understand it. I was a bit disoriented by it. But I just let it sit and then as I engaged and worked and spent time there I saw what the definition meant.

It's not just walking through [Country] – it's actually being there, being back on a place that knows you. You're in a real relationship with it. I really enjoyed this shift in my thinking because, training as a landscape architect, I had a very prescriptive kind of methodology around site assessment and landscape types, so they fit very distinct pieces and that was just a scientific definition. There wasn't any social science in that. And that's one of things that I think is really beautiful about gardening – it encompasses so many layers of social science which is really what Aboriginal and Torres Strait culture is. It's science that goes through the head and through the heart. And our science is all head and anything too heart is deemed wishy-washy and airy-fairy. Whereas their connection to science is housed in the heart and the story and they synthesise those two so beautifully. And you realise that heart and head storytelling has prevailed to pass on incredible knowledge without libraries, without stenographers, books, CDs, blah blah blah.

Costa went on to talk about how he was at an event earlier that day where he witnessed Aboriginal and Torres Strait Islander people mixing up soil and painting their bodies with it.

That's about putting the earth on you to absorb into you and that's your way to connect. So in a similar way, gardening and getting your hands in the soil is this chance to actually put your DNA – or have the DNA of where you are – rub up against you and actually have your hands in where you are.

That's a solid reason for not wearing gardening gloves! With your hands in the soil your DNA can be in relationship with the DNA of the land you're on.

Australian Aboriginal cuisine is the oldest in the world. Down here in Lutruwita/Tasmania, Palawa woman Kitana Mansell runs palawa kipli. This Aboriginal owned and operated enterprise offers Aboriginal and Torres Strait catering for events.

I think that the community loves that palawa kipli is Aboriginal owned and operated and that we've finally got our own foot in our own industry that we've created as Aboriginal people. And they even love that I've been able to turn our palawa kipli cuisine into something a bit more fancy. Usually we just have mutton birds from the BBQ and we're just eating them all with our hands, all messy. But then I can create these really elegant dishes that really bring out the flavours by cooking it in like a native honey and cooking it on the fire and we're breaking that down so you've got nice little pieces, just so create new and exciting dishes but they're still the base of what our traditional food is.

So it's great to see the responses from the community, that they're just so excited for the journey that I've been on with my community to get the word out there on many different shows and national shows that we never thought we'd even get our names on the map of, so it's great to really have Aboriginal people from our community represent our foods finally.

While Kitana didn't grow up knowing her native plants she was drawn to gardening because of the impacts of colonisation.

We don't see many of our native plants growing on our lands anymore. Without native plants our world cannot continue to be sustainable and [we can't] continue to thrive as Aboriginal people: to still continue having our medicines, our food and just being able to care for Country and to have that connection to what's growing in our soils to who we are as people.

Any traditional food of ours, we're just all trying to bring that back to the forefront of Aboriginal culture and practice. Just with colonisation after the past 250 years, a lot of that's all becoming non-Aboriginal industries now … So we really have to take charge now before it's too late to protect all of these species and plants and then show them the right way to make it a sustainable industry before we don't have any of it left.

Kitana's hope for the future is one where Aboriginal people live and eat their traditional foods again. Not just every now and then, but daily. By reconnecting with their plants and their foods, they can connect with their living history. '[We need to] really reconnect back to our food again because it plays such a role in our health. [We] have very low life expectancy, so it will also create a healthier community if we started learning more and getting more involved in these foods.'

For Kitana, just as with Bruce, gardening on whatever land is available is a step in the right direction of nourishing culture, reclaiming sovereignty and caring for Country.

Holding onto culture

Any time you listen to or watch the news or are on social media, you will be able to witness people in real time being displaced from their homelands. Global conflict is rife and it's ripping people's lives and homes apart, killing countless innocent people. Horrifying doesn't come close to describing the impacts of such violent displacement.

It's this violence and the urge to survive that forces millions of people to flee their homelands, becoming refugees or internally displaced people. They leave their homes to find a safer existence. Often travelling by foot, they carry only the essentials and, for those who have access to them, this includes seeds. This is partly so they can establish food gardens wherever they're going so they can eat. But there's also something else stored in those seeds.

In 2012, Aveen Ismail fled Damascus Syria) with her family and settled in Domiz, one of the biggest camps in Kurdistan, Northern Iraq and home to 30,000 refugees. Here most of the refugees were from Syria and one of the key things they packed when fleeing were seeds. Aveen says, 'Creating a garden was a way for us to heal and remind us of home.'[53] Interestingly, but not surprisingly, not all the gardens were full of food. Roses and other flowers also featured – food for the soul.

Alfonso Montiel of the Lemon Tree Trust worked in Domiz for several years. 'They want seeds from their own plants, from their own spaces, from their own families,' he said.[54] They want to feel connected to their culture, to where they've come from and to who they are. Seeds and gardens can play a role in doing just this.

Mahatma Gandhi once said, 'To forget how to dig the earth and to tend the soil is to forget ourselves.' From India, Gandhi trained as a lawyer before becoming a prominent anti-colonial activist and political ethicist famous for his non-violent protests. He led what became the successful campaign against Britain for Indian independence and influenced civil rights movements around the world. While far from being saint-like (as he's sometimes presented), his connection to people, place and culture and commitment to working for India's freedom is undeniable. Part of his advocacy included holistic education that provided both academic and practical skills relevant to everyday life so that India's vast rural population could be empowered to sustain themselves. This included craft, gardening and agriculture.[55]

While Syrian refugees fleeing their homes packed seeds for food security and to hold onto a sense of home, culture and self, Gandhi advocated for practical such as like gardening to be embedded into education as a form of civil resistance to British rule so they too could hold onto a sense of home, culture and self. Both cultures were (and still are) remembering themselves with the help of gardening.

Grounding yourself

Tim Winton said, 'It seems obvious to the point of embarrassment, but I guess you'd have to say [gardening is] grounding.'

This is a sentiment often highlighted by people who move across the world (voluntarily or not) and arrive in a feeling that's the opposite to being grounded – floaty, untethered and anxious, looking to grasp onto the familiar. The tangible act of digging, planting, composting, pruning, mulching and watering can lead to intangible benefits including feeling grounded or calm in yourself and more connected with where you are, but also where you've come from. It's a way to keep treasured memories alive, while also building new memories and new communities.

- For Johanna, who hails from Germany and now lives in Australia, gardening helps keep a living connection to her home country alive: 'Gardening helps me to feel closer to home, and to my mum, who is an amazing gardener. I noticed that I mainly plant plants that my mum has in her garden, basically recreating my childhood garden a little bit.' To squeeze more into their urban garden, Johanna has taken up grafting: 'Our apricot now has a branch of German prune, and our nectarine has about six varieties of prune and plum, including the French ones my mum has in her garden.'
- Becky grew up in the Shetland Isles (an archipelago in Scotland): 'At twelve years old, I established a veggie garden on an island in the middle of the North Sea, and to date, I haven't been able to grow cauliflowers as good!' She moved to Australia twenty years ago. 'My veggie garden connects

me back to my childhood and school holiday visits to my grandparents who had an amazing veggie garden. They ate from the garden every evening. I wish they could see my garden now; the time they spent with me back then is part of the very threads of my being.'

- A different Becky grew up in the West Country of England (Devon and Cornwall) in a family of passionate gardeners. As a child she would shovel cow pats in the fields with her grandad and wheelbarrow them back for her mum's roses. 'I remember the thrill of digging for potatoes with him and the intoxicating scent of his sweet peas.' These days she lives in Nipaluna/Hobart. 'I do think back to my English family when I am gardening – remembering their pearls of wisdom. I imagine them being proud of me continuing the gardening tradition and shocked at the differences between their gardens and mine. So yes, gardening does keep me connected mentally with my original home and culture … A love of gardening connects us all, wherever we are in the world.'

- When Amelia moved to Japan she lived in an international student dorm. 'There was all this land in the back and horse stables next door and autumn leaves on campus and I was offered the back oval to turn into a community permaculture garden. I desperately missed community gardening. It turned into this magical place where international women students would gather every Friday and we'd grow veg and herbs and we grew Japanese varieties of things, but experiment cooking dishes from our homes with bits and pieces that we grew. There were women who'd never touched soil or seen a worm before.

At a time when I was soooooooo homesick, and so were the other girls, we found companionship and connection in this garden together.'

When I moved properly to Lutruwita/Tasmania by myself (after visiting for years), I struggled to find new gardening friends. I'd just moved from (r)Adelaide where I had been surrounded by urban agriculture kindred souls. Suddenly I was on an island, disconnected from my gardening community. I was very lonely in those first few months.

That was until I found David Stephen. He was already in his sixties by then, but fitter than me and with the most sparkly and delightful blue eyes. We became quick and easy friends thanks to our shared obsession with edible gardens. We spent years building community and school gardens together. He helped me with my own garden and would even turn up at compost workshops I was teaching and heckle me (which I loved). Rumour has it that the late legendary Peter Cundall called David one of the best gardeners in Tasmania – I believe it. Every patch of earth he touches is transformed into an overachieving edible garden and his compost is the stuff of love and life. Meeting David made me feel like my new island life was going to be okay. And all because I'd found a friend and a garden.

Wherever you end up in the world, gardening can follow you. Like a friend you didn't even know you had or needed, it's there to comfort you and remind you that wherever you are, you're at home, both in yourself and on the earth.

- '[I garden] for the feelings and the connecting. Connecting with myself, connecting with the earth and nature, connecting with joy and excitement and satisfaction, connecting with my creativity, connecting with memories and people who have gone, connecting with and sharing with others.' **Claire M**

As activism

Sometimes
we forget
That the only
thing stopping
Our freedom
is us

Something I believe in passionately is gardening's ability to be a form of solution-based activism. It's no exaggeration to say that gardening can help address some of the big challenges of our times including equal access to land, climate change, food security, pollution and mental and physical human health. It's particularly powerful when people work together; this is when its capacity to push back on business as usual is most effective. And sometimes, contrary to what you might imagine when you think of activism, you can tackle these big issues while having fun in the process!

An example … I have a habit of reading research and strategic reports from local and state government that are relevant to my work, including ones that cover health, waste and food. This is how I learned the extent of how bad things are in Lurtuwita/Tasmania in terms of equality access to healthy food:

Tasmania has one of the highest rates of obesity, diabetes and heart disease in the country. One of the reasons is that, for many people, it isn't easy to access healthy food. In fact, data suggest that up to 30 per cent of Tasmanians are affected by poor access to nutritious, affordable food, and that resulting health care costs the state around $60 million per year.[56]

In response to learning this, I applied for and received a local urban sustainability grant and initiated what became known as the Home Harvest event.[57] This is an annual self-guided edible garden tour in and around Nipaluna/Hobart. The aim is to showcase what's possible on urban properties of all shapes and sizes. This free event sees many hundreds of people exposed to edible landscapes, reminding them that cityscapes are still landscapes and that they can use their land (or balconies with pots) to grow some of the food they need to thrive. They're able to come look, learn and leave inspired to start or keep going with edible gardening. Over the years, I've received dozens of messages from people saying that thanks to that event they've started or expanded their edible gardens, which in turn improves their health and food security.

To make this event happen, I successfully applied for a local grant for five years in a row, hoping the funding body wouldn't notice I was just doing the same thing again and again. The sixth year, they called me up and said, 'Hannah, we can't keep giving you this grant.' I was disappointed but not surprised. But their next sentence *did* surprise me. They said that instead of giving me the grant, they'd decided to integrate the project into their core funding for the next few years! They recognised that it was meeting key parts of their strategic plan to increase food security and improve health and urban sustainability.

This is solution-based activism: seeing the problem, identifying the opportunities and making things happen until they help shift the cultural dial so they're normalised.

Costa agrees: 'Really hardcore, strategic outcomes can be achieved under the banner of gardening ... Confrontation is needed to shift certain paradigms, but it can't be the only tool in the toolbox. Otherwise people will just isolate and turn off.'

There are so many different types of activism. I call my personal flavour of activism solution-based activism and gardening plays a central role in it. I like this approach in particular as it identifies and addresses big challenges in the world (think climate change) but in a way that doesn't dwell on the problem. Instead it dwells on the solutions. I use positive, fun activities to engage people in the solutions to show them that another life is not only possible, but it is delightful, fulfilling and very much within our power to create. This is my jam.

Some folks might think activism is a dirty word, but activism just means you care enough to help bring about political or social change towards a certain goal. It means you're paying attention to the world and that you care very deeply. You can be an activist for conservative or progressive causes (I'm the latter in case you haven't noticed). For me, activism and caring for the land go together like red wriggler worms and warm horse poo.

Gardening and farming can be both a form of resistance and a call for something more. And this is exactly what you can see looking through time: people engaging in all forms of gardening as a physical form of activism, using their bodies to shape a different way of being in, and relating to, the world.

Here's what Costa thinks about activism:

I sometimes look at the big picture of the world and go, well, I'm just one more blip, and that blip could easily take the approach of 'I can't make a difference.' Or that blip could say 'How can we do things to make a buffer, and make insurance for what may or may not happen?' I'm not going to allow the negativity and the narrative of that reality to bring me down. Because I feel it's incumbent on me, personally, to do what I can to make the world a better place for my god kids, and great nieces and nephews and kids.

He doesn't call it this, but I see Costa's work as a wonderful example of solution-based activism. Over the years of working alongside him and watching him in action I've seen that he always keeps it real, finds the common ground and crafts connections between everyone seamlessly.

I'm deliberately optimistic, not because someone tells me to be, *but because I see it* – the good work that's been done. And if I can amplify that to find a place in people [so they can] take that and do what's appropriate for them, then that's not being optimistic. It's me being prescriptive and saying "look at this" and "look at that" … My opportunity is more to disseminate information … to disturb, engage and inspire.

I see too much good stuff [not] to know there's momentum. I know there's also [negative] momentum on the other side of the fence, but I feel that being able to share with people the good things can help counter the [other] momentum that I can't stand in front of cause they'll roll over me. But I can alter and affect it by having many people being affected by the positive side.

Fighting for food security

Perhaps one of the more well-known forms of activist gardening is guerrilla gardening. The term was first used in relation to the group Green Guerrillas in the 1970s in America. Founded by Liz Christy, Amos Taylor and Martin Gallent the group would throw what we now call 'seed bombs' over fences into vacant lots to greenify their dilapidated neighbourhood in the Bowery Houston area of New York. They eventually established Bowery Houston Farm and Garden, now known as the Liz Christy Garden, and began community organising to use public gardening as 'a tool to reclaim urban land, stabilise city blocks, and get people working together to solve problems'. Co-founder Amos Taylor said that 'it was a form of civil disobedience – we were basically saying to the government, if you won't do it, we will.'[58]

You'll see this attitude all over the world – people saying 'Fuck it! If the people in power aren't going to do anything, I will.' My dad's like that. All through my childhood he was prone to a spot of nighttime guerrilla gardening, planting native trees on empty lots and verges. For him, actions speak louder than words. I'm reminded of the quote from Wangari Maathai: 'Until you dig a hole, you plant a tree, you water it and make it survive, you haven't done a thing. You are just talking.'[59]

I remember during my childhood the delight of seeing a new tree appear in the neighbouring empty lot – like a gradual unveiling of treasure. As I grew up, so did the trees until they were big enough for me to climb. On my rare trips back to that neighbourhood I can still spot a few of the trees, but alas most have been removed in the name of development. And yeah, that sucks – but it would suck even more if they never happened, if those patches of land were just left unloved for the decades my family lived there. I reckon it's always best to love the land you're on at any opportunity.

Guerrilla gardening, like the type my dad practised in the streets of West End, isn't a new thing. While it didn't have the snappy name it has now, you can swoop back in time to see it in action throughout history. During the 1500s to 1800s, colonising forces swept across African countries. Farmers were enslaved and taken to the Americas. Before they were forcibly removed from their land, they braided seeds into their hair as means to hold on to what was most dear – a sense of self, home and food security.[60] Once in the Americas they created secret gardens on marginal land. Scholar Geri Augusto elaborates:

> Enslaved people took the initiative … to create small plots and provision grounds … either beside the slave hut or [on] a piece of land that the plantation owner didn't need. [T]hey would raise vegetables, medicinal plants, and even flowers. In a way, you can think of it as part of resistance – survival is always resistance if you can make it … They were supplementing their diet, but also it was a small, small patch in which they could be human.[61]

Meanwhile, in 1649 in England, a group called the Diggers rose up against the British aristocracy to try and reclaim their land. The aristocracy had been busy locking up land that common folk had previously relied on for food and fuel. The Diggers started planting edible crops on a prominent hillside to draw attention to the resulting malnutrition crisis. While it was short lived, they made a strong statement. It didn't change things immediately, but it contributed to the longer conversation of access to and autonomy over land.[62]

This sentiment is wrapped up in the term 'food sovereignty', which was popularised in 1993 by La Via Campesina. An international movement representing around 200 million peasant small-scale producers from 180 local and national organisations in eighty-one countries, La Via Campesina champions the rights of producers and promotes ecologically sound land management. According to its website:

> Food Sovereignty is the right of peoples to healthy and culturally appropriate food produced through ecologically sound and sustainable methods and their right to define their food and agriculture systems. La Via Campesina insists that diverse, peasant-driven agroecological modes of production, based on centuries of experience and accumulated evidence, are central to guaranteeing healthy food to everyone while remaining in harmony with nature. To achieve food sovereignty, La Via Campesina mobilises and advocates for agrarian reform in peasant territories and provides training on agroecological production methods.[63]

In 2018, after seventeen years of persistent lobbying and advocacy by La Via Campesina, the United Nations adopted the Declaration on Rights of Peasants and Other People Working in Rural Areas. This declaration is an important tool in ensuring small-scale producers are defended and that food sovereignty is implemented.

You see, when people can't access land and don't have control over their food system they lose autonomy over their quality of life. No one knows this more than Indian eco-activist and scholar Dr Vandana Shiva. While she has a PhD in quantum physics, Shiva has dedicated her life to advocating against an industrial, centralised agriculture model and for a decentralised, organic and ecologically sound agriculture movement with food sovereignty at its heart: 'This industrialised globalised system of food is destroying soil, it is destroying water and it is generating 30 per cent of our greenhouse gasses. If we want to fix this, we've got to shift from industrial to ecological farming.'[64]

She has worked tirelessly to protect farmers' rights to access and plant traditional seeds in the face of global corporations who want to patent them. This has included travelling extensively across India, collecting and saving seeds (including 4000 varieties of rice), teaching farmers how to return to organic practices, establishing at least 100 seed banks and setting up Navdanya, 'an earth centric, women centric and farmer led movement for the protection of biological and cultural diversity.'[65] They have a membership of 6.5 million farmer families and grow and save thousands seeds and provide education to support people to grow organically.

These examples throughout history of gardening as a form of social justice are one of the many reasons I grow a garden and grow a food garden in particular. While I grew up in a gardening family in an urban herb nursery, it wasn't until I started learning about global politics, climate change and food sovereignty that I realised that gardening can be a form of activism. I asked Tim Winton what he thought about this concept and he explained that, for him, 'Food gardens can be a form of resistance – not just to isolation or despair, but to the isolating and pitiless logic of capitalism. Anyone who shares their surplus with family, friends and neighbours and receives surplus of other sorts in return understands this.'

I understand this deeply. When I grow food and share it with friends or pop surplus produce into our local food share stand (an old bookshelf out the front of a friend's house), it's a direct action against industrial agriculture and capitalism and a direct action for a local, regenerative and resilient food system that puts people and planet before profit. These might seem like small gestures, but they are just a few of the many ways that gardening can be a force for good and a useful addition to the activism toolbox.

Grassroots movements

Someone else who understands the connection between gardening and activism is my mate David Stephen. David, along with permaculture co-originator the late Bill Mollison and original *Gardening Australia* host the late Peter Cundall helped popularise the organic gardening movement in Australia in the 1970s. David explained to me how the movement took shape. Mollison was busy galvanising people around the concept of setting up a consumer's co-op that included developing 'repair stations' – a place where you could repair broken goods to give them new life and promote sustainability. Hundreds of people signed up to be part of it and together they set up a shop front from which to sell organic produce. The only problem was that they couldn't find people who were growing organic produce.

This is where David came in. He was one of the few organic gardeners around. He hosted a public meeting to address the lack of organic gardens and to introduce the term 'organic gardening' to help promote and normalise it. 'Twelve people turned up, including Peter Cundall, and as chairman of the meeting I very soon had to sit down because Peter just took over,' David says. I asked David if this was a good thing or hard thing, to which he replied, 'Oh thank goodness! 'Cause I could hardly put two sentences together.'

Following this meeting, the Australia Organic Gardening Society was established with a number of branches set up across Lutruwita/ Tasmania. David opened one in Nipaluna/Hobart and Peter Cundall opened one in Launceston before hitting the road to open more around the island, including on the West Coast, Swansea and New Norfolk.

'I went to one of those meetings in New Norfolk (southern Tasmania),' recalls David. 'It was so full they were hanging from the rafters listening to every word – because Peter Cundall had quite a personal following … We became the largest organic gardening movement in the world per capita according to Lawrence Hills, a British global leader in organic gardening who came to visit.'

The work that David Stephen, Peter Cundall and Bill Mollison did in the 1970s helped fuel the popular organic garden movement which is still growing strong today. Their grassroots education campaign sparked generations of gardeners into organic practices and rippled across the globe.

Grassroots campaigns are often part of progressive movements. In 2008 in a small town called Todmorden in the United Kingdom, a group of mates got together to beautify the unloved areas of their town with edible gardens. Their aim was to reconnect folks with Nature and with each other. And so Incredible Edible Todmorden was born.[66] Over the years they've worked with local schools to establish edible landscapes, set up a tool library, and run regular workshops and weekly working bees. The police house in Todmorden is now famous for its garden! It's become a popular photo location for the tourists who come from all over the world to admire, learn and get inspired. The movement has no paid staff, no buildings and no public funding. They like to think that what they're doing is radical community building in action.[67]

And then there's my old friend Jen Calder who co-established

Source Community Wholefoods on the campus of the University of Tasmania. This is where I first met her, over planning meetings for the community garden and a strawbale co-op that formed part of the project. This project (which is still going) was all about empowering the community – taking power away from the big two supermarkets and putting it back into community hands. At the same time, the project promoted sustainable farming and reduced food packaging. While we received some grants and lots of in-kind support, the Source Community Wholefoods only happened because a grassroots community formed to bring it to life through years of voluntary work. The government and industry weren't doing anything ... *so we did it ourselves.*

Meanwhile, in Meanjin/Brisbane, a group of volunteers established Growing Forward, a movement that creates community gardens on vacant lots and underutilised public land throughout the city. It's a more radical version of community gardens, one where you ask for forgiveness instead of permission from authorities to establish the garden. When I was up in Meanjin/Brisbane, I went on a self-guided tour through one of their gardens: Kurilpa Commons in West End. Free-styling veggies and perennial crops blended with flowers frolicking through the space. Signage encourages anyone and everyone to help themselves. No one was there to welcome me, but I felt completely welcome. While they might be bending the rules, Growing Forward is achieving so much by utilising gardening as activism. Not only are they providing free food to those in need, they are also engaging people in bigger conversations about access to land, food security and community resilience as a human right. And accessing a human right isn't something we should have to ask permission for.

Why gardeners also need wild spaces

Many of the passionate environmentalists I've met over decades are also avid gardeners or farmers. It's not just because they like the look of plants in their gardens or local forests (although they do). It's because they understand that you can't have your backyard oasis or thriving farmscape without wild ecosystems also thriving. Most of us know that humanity needs wild spaces, but we may not realise that our gardens need them, too – and by extension our whole food system.

To survive and thrive, we rely on the biggest gardens on earth; I'm talking about our wild places such as old growth forests, vast grasslands, coastal ecosystems and marine wonderlands. We need clean water for irrigation, topsoil for growing, trees to capture carbon from the atmosphere and sequester it into the ground, and seaweed to do the same in our oceans, and insects and wildlife to maintain balance. We can only have this type of holistic health when our wild places are preserved and under good management involving Aboriginal and Torres Strait Islander peoples. This last point is important: when we give land back, we're also supporting the process of Aboriginal and Torres Strait Islander peoples getting their culture back.

As a passionate gardener, I am also a passionate environmentalist. That's why I'm into my third decade supporting the ongoing campaign to protect old growth forests in Lutruwita/Tasmania. Over the years I've peacefully sat in front of bulldozers, climbed up tree sits, marched the streets, donated cash, volunteered to support political campaigns and run half marathons (slowly) through Takayna/the Tarkine rainforest to raise funds and awareness. I do all this because I know the health of my backyard plot depends on the health of the broader ecosystem. Where I live in Lutruwita/Tasmania, the broader ecosystem includes forests such as Takayna/Tarkine, but also river systems, grasslands, open woodlands, coastal regions and alpine areas. Together they support the diversity of flora and fauna, filter water and build soil health. Sure, we could still have a garden if we log and mine forests or compromise other ecosystems. But the reduction of wildlife (including precious insects) and the likelihood of increased pollution in the ground, water and air would significantly compromise how healthy our garden might be.

Takayna/the Tarkine is the largest temperate rainforest in Australia and the second largest in the world. If we lose it to mining and logging (the current threat), we would lose not only incredible biodiversity and Aboriginal cultural heritage, but also a carbon sink that can hold over 100 million tonnes of carbon in the ground.[68]

But what does that mean exactly? It means that a healthy forest can sequester carbon in the soil 'by capturing carbon dioxide from the atmosphere and transforming it into biomass through photosynthesis. Sequestered carbon is then accumulated in the form of biomass, deadwood, litter and in forest soils.'[69] In plain speak this means a forest can suck carbon dioxide (aka greenhouse gas) from the atmosphere and turn it into plant matter and soil. By 'locking it up' in the ground it is not doing harm in the atmosphere where it would contribute to climate change.

And as Bob Brown says, 'As intact native forests across the globe become rarer, secure protection of Takayna's forests are a key component in mitigating global climate change.'[70]

The bottom line is that forests such as Takayna/Tarkine are increasingly rare and incredibly vital for ecosystem and human health. If we want a stable and safe climate to live and garden in, we need these ecosystems protected and/or restored.

Rebellious hope

Gardening also gives us hope that another world is possible. Jude Bennet was a young teenager when he first appeared as a guest presenter on ABC TV's *Gardening Australia*. He explains that he gardens 'because it grounds me in this crazy, chaotic world as it is a physical thing I can act on to improve the environment around me and my community. Gardening gives me the confidence and hope to do the other important things in my life.'

A gardener from my online survey contributed this beauty:

'In a time of climate fear and a lack of control over the big decisions, gardening is my soul food and feels like an act of rebellious hope. I'm in a position of privilege so feel a responsibility to grow to share.' **Katie T**

I asked my old gardening mate David Stephen if gardening gives him hope for the world. In true David form, he quickly snapped 'No, I think the world's stuffed.' David doesn't believe in beating around the bush. 'But I must be optimistic because I keep going and teaching, but eventually I think we won't get very far.' These were harsh words for me to hear, but understandable given our global trajectory. I nudged him to tell me why he bothers gardening and he landed on the conclusion that there is something like hope there, because not doing something isn't an option. And this is where he and I meet – in the 'doing something' space, which is exactly the space where activism grows. It's turning your values, your core beliefs into real-life actions that make a dent in the world in the best possible way you know how.

There's a concept I hold onto tightly called radical or active hope.[71] This is not the type of hope where you send your thoughts and prayers towards a better future. It's the type of hope where you roll your sleeves up and get busy living a different future into reality. It's messy, relentless and non-linear. It hurts, it's hard and it requires you to be tenacious and hustle for something better and fairer.

It's about carving out new pathways towards just outcomes for the common good. The alternative is to do nothing ... and that just isn't a viable or sensible choice. I'm a firm believer that the only option is to embrace our collective power to push for cultural change that puts people and planet firmly before profit and power.

Gardening with an activist lens can be a form of powerful and radical active hope towards a just future. Whether it's reclaiming public land for the common good, storing carbon in the ground or remembering that we are Nature, gardening can play an important role in pointing you in the right direction.

The examples of activism shared in this chapter are all from wildly different places of the world, from different times in history, cultures, contexts and on different scales. But look closer and there are a couple of common threads.

Firstly, everyone is seeking land (for gardening or ecosystem health) to survive and thrive. The connection between healthy people, culture and thriving landscapes is inextricably linked.

The second thread I can see is people pushing back on authority and the accepted dominating culture of the time. This happens when people's way of life or actual lives are under threat and when their values are being compromised or obliterated.

And finally, running through every example in this chapter is a sense of intergenerational justice. That what we do today with our gardens and landscapes will determine the viability and health of future generations' lives. Activist gardening is both a gift to ourselves now, but it's also a carefully wrapped present for the future. We're saying, I can see there's more to this global picture of life than my own experience and that what is outside my personal sphere and beyond my life matters. That it (the future) deserves my precious time, my clear attention and my full heart to ensure that it has a chance of existing to its full potential and sparkling glory.

And this, dear readers, is where we get to my favourite bit of the book: where I get to share the concept of being a Time Rebel with you.

To time travel

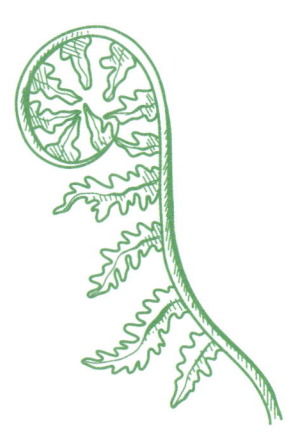

Planting
trees today
For our
grandchildren
to climb
Laughing in
their shade

I first heard of the term Time Rebel in 2022 and tracked it down to social philosopher Roman Krznaric. Time Rebels are people who are 'dedicated to intergenerational justice and long-term thinking'.[72] They're focused on countering the plague of short-term thinking that currently rules our dominant politics and culture globally. The type of thinking that's based on election cycles or how much money an industry can make in that year. This kind of thinking has a nasty habit of sidestepping what's best for the collective good in favour of what's best for personal bank accounts and missions for power. Time Rebels are bending time (travelling through it, if you like). They know that everything we do today has been informed by the past and will be felt for generations to come.

What's this got to do with gardening? Well, I'm interested in the story we tell ourselves when we're pottering around our backyards. Are we thinking about building soil health for future generations, about sharing hands-on knowledge and skills with our community and whether the people who come after us will benefit? Or are we thinking about whether this is even worth our time, our resources and how it'd be more efficient to just go buy the thing from the shops? Often it's the latter (hell, even I've had that thought occasionally). But without fail I always return to the knowledge that what we do now, in our short lives, not only impacts those around us but also those who come after us. For me, gardening is one way of being a Time Rebel – the knowing the soil health I build and the skills I foster around gardening and landscape care and the stories I share have the potential to help people beyond my lifetime. I'm bending time by investing in present-day actions that benefit the future. Action that can add to the collective ripples other Time Rebels are making, ripples that have the potential to be felt for generations to come.

Importantly, while Time Rebel is a newish term, it's old thinking that embraces intergenerational relationships and thinking that you'll find in Indigenous cultures across the world.

An ancient philosophy

In Indigenous Australia there's a somewhat similar concept that is described with different words in different Aboriginal languages. One of which is Jukurrpa, used by several groups in the Central Desert region. In English this is commonly and inadequately known as the Dreaming or the Dreamtime. Jukurrpa 'is seen as going from the past to the present to the future all at once, so it is something that sits outside ordinary timelines'.[73]

Jukurrpa is also known as Altyerrenge or Altyerr by the Arrerntic peoples, Ngarrankarni by the Kija people of the East Kimberley, Ungud (or Wungud) by the Ngarinyin people and some in Northeast Arnhem Land refer to the concept as Wongar.[74] And there's more – this is a small sample to indicate the diversity and complexity in language.

Dr Christine Nicholls spent over a decade living at Lajamanu, a remote Warlpiri Aboriginal settlement in the Tanami Desert of the Northern Territory. Here she worked as a linguist, learning several local Aboriginal languages and later becoming the local school's principal. She writes about Jukurrpa:

> As a religion grounded in the land itself, it incorporates creation and other land-based narratives, social processes including kinship regulations, morality and ethics. This complex concept informs people's economic, cognitive, affective and spiritual lives'.
>
> The Dreaming embraces time past, present and future, a substantively different concept from populist characterisations portraying it as 'timeless' or having taken place at the so-called 'dawn of time'. Unfortunately, even in mainstream Australia today, when and where we should know better, schmaltzy, quasi-New Age notions of 'The Dreaming' frequently still hold sway.[75]

The Australian anthropologist WEH Stanner conveyed the idea more accurately in his germinal 1956 essay 'The Dreaming'[76], in which he coined the term 'everywhen'. 'One cannot "fix" The Dreaming in time: it was, and is, everywhen' wrote Stanner, adding that the Dreaming 'has … an unchallengeable sacred authority'.

Stanner went on to observe that 'We [non-Indigenous Australians] shall not understand The Dreaming fully except as a *complex of meanings*'.[77]

A complex of meanings that weave in and out of time, through past, present and future.

In Aotearoa/New Zealand, Anna-Maria Murtola and Shannon Walsh are Maori writers and descendants of Ngāpuhi, a Maori iwi or social group, from Te Tai Tokerau, the Northland Region of New Zealand. They explain that in traditional Māori culture there's a term called whakapapa.

[This concept] explains the origins, positioning, and futures of all things. Whakapapa derives from the root 'papa', meaning a base or foundation. Whakapapa denotes a layering, adding to that foundation. Rooted in creation, generations layer upon each other, creating a reality of intergenerational relationships. Everything has whakapapa, all phenomena, spiritual and physical, from celestial bodies, days and nights, through to the winds, lands, waters, and all that transpires throughout.[78]

... each generation coexists like droplets immersed in the ocean of time. Knowledge of whakapapa allows us to navigate the intergenerational currents that constitute this ocean of never-ending beginnings. Through onamata, anamata each generation can traverse these waters, put down an anchor, and take in the view. This is a Māori futurism.[79]

I like the idea of being able to throw down your anchor to take in the view of your cultural context, seeing all that went before, all that is in the present, knowing that it's linked to everything that will come. It gives you the perspective that what you do now has significance and is linked to a bigger story. That your contribution to the story can help shape the narrative.

In Norway, the Future Library[80] is a project that has traces of Time Rebel-ness to it. Each year the Future Library Trust selects an author of significance to contribute a manuscript which won't be revealed until one hundred years later (starting in 2014 this will be 2114). But wait, there's more! A forest was planted in 2014 and will be harvested in 2114 to make the paper for these manuscripts to be printed on. The Future Library Trust signed a one-hundred agreement with the City of Oslo and has systems in place to facilitate a project of this length.

How wonderful! They're gardening with trees now so that art can happen later; thinking beyond their lifetimes to do good things when they're long gone and weaving links of connection through multiple generations in the process.

'The true meaning of life is to plant trees,
under whose shade you do not expect to sit.'
– Nelson Henderson

Many gardeners naturally employ this long-term thinking. They're thinking about the trees they plant which might not mature for decades, possibly until after they're gone. They're thinking about their children and how homegrown food and connection to Nature will benefit them into adulthood. They're thinking about saving heirloom seeds that have been passed down for generations and sharing them with their own gardening networks for all time. They're always thinking about soil health and often choosing not to use harmful chemicals on their patches to ensure they're building ecosystem health for decades to come. And increasingly, gardeners and farmers are thinking about climate change and food security. They're thinking about how they have to moderate their growing practices to respond to it and they're thinking about how their gardens and farms can help counter the effects of climate change that we're already seeing. This type of thinking is Time Rebel thinking. Gardeners are acting now on behalf of the future.

- 'It provides a positive way to individually respond to the climate crisis and growing pesticide-free organic produce.' **Kate Smallwood**
- 'I feel like I am taking action on the climate crisis and flipping the middle finger to a disconnected, capitalist, individualist way of living.' **Sam G**
- 'Gardening allows me to make a small difference in a changing world. Improving the soil and habitat in my garden helps me feel positive about the future.' **Anonymous**
- 'Growing my own food reminds me every day how my existence is intrinsically linked to the land. Humans are not apart from nature, they ARE nature. My native garden is a way of restoring natural processes that have been lost post-colonisation. And mostly, all of this brings me HOPE in the face of the climate crisis.' **Jessica Holding**
- 'Gardening is a tangible, visible act of courage and hope in the face of climate crisis.' **Enken**
- 'Ecological gardening practices and growing some of my own food reduces my personal feelings of helplessness in the face of existential climate crisis by offering a little bit of agency.' **Rachel Summers**
- 'As a school kitchen garden teacher, I garden to ignite the joy and love of gardening and sustainability to the next generation.' **Rosemary Everingham**
- 'To build skills as a community for the future we want to create – solidarity, direct democracy, working together to

each of our abilities to provide for each other's needs. To rebuild social relations damaged by capitalism/colonialism. Being in relationship with community (human and non-human) gives me hope and joy!' **Anonymous**

• 'It is a link to the past times with my grandparents, present with my daughter and a small action for the future.' **Anonymous**

As I get older I've come to understand the importance of fostering relationships with people of all ages. I get a particular kick of joy meeting younger gardeners such as Jude Bennett who lives and gardens in the Blue Mountains, New South Wales. Jude took up gardening when he was twelve in 2020 during Covid-19 lockdowns when schools closed and gatherings were not allowed. His passion for it got him a guest gig on ABC TV's *Gardening Australia*. What started as one row of snow peas along the fence line quickly blew out into a massive patch once the edible rewards got their tendrils into him. Within eighteen months he was feeding his family as much as they could eat and selling surplus to local shops.

As well as his own garden, Jude has spent time volunteering with local project Farm It Forward[81] which runs mini market gardens on unused land. Founder Manu Prigioni says Jude 'provides us with this incredible hope for the future because he shows us that a lot of our young people are really passionate about growing regeneratively and feeding communities locally.'[82]

The thing about hope is that it doesn't spontaneously occur in a vacuum. It erupts when one caring heart meets another caring heart. We recognise each other's efforts towards something better for ourselves and for those yet to come. It's in this spark of recognition that hope lurches into the world. And this is how we can help keep each other going, through time.

With edible gardening being of particular interest to Jude it wasn't long before we connected, first by email (via his rad mum Mary), then in real life. Jude and some of his family visited me and my garden when they came to Lutruwita/Tasmania on a holiday. We drank tea, walked around my garden and shared a meal together. It was pure delight.

Mary mentioned something along the lines of how good it was to have a role model like me for Jude to look up to. But it's a two-way thing – Jude's a role model for me too. Through his actions, he instils deep hope in me that humanity will keep turning up determined to grow a better world for all.

This all feeds into the concept of being a Time Rebel, which encourages us to build relationships with people of all ages so that we can understand each other's lived experiences. But it also involves building relationships with people through time – with our shared ancestors and with those who are yet to be born.

I use the term 'shared ancestors' to broaden our minds to include people we're not related to by blood, rather people we're related to through a shared love of humanity and ecosystem health. I've picked up the baton from where they left off and am continuing or evolving their work, progressing things for the next generation to do the same. This thinking has given me a new perspective; it's taught me that the work I'm part of, in and out of the garden, is long-game, multigenerational work. It's unlikely we'll solve the big problems of our times in our short lives, but the more we try, the more good we're doing for future generations. Time Rebels work hard now, using their lives as a precious gift for future generations to come.

It's important to note that Time Rebel thinking isn't confined to the garden. When we bring Time Rebel thinking to big collective decision-making such as how we vote, we can impact our environment, economic framework or cultural setting with timeless thinking that will benefit future generations and not just the now. We can ask ourselves, how would future generations like me to cast my vote? What would benefit them and not just me? Fostering this intergenerational connection can result in real-world outcomes, such as who runs our country!

I believe the foundation of being a Time Rebel is based on the understanding that we have a connection with all living things across time. And that when you're connected to something, you care for it. Building relationships across generations with connection and care upfront is crucial to building a vibrant future.

All this relates directly to why I garden. When you garden, you're building a relationship with the land you live on, the life that grows from it and the wildlife that interacts with it. Just like you learn to read the lines on a loved one's face, I've learned how to read my landscape in a way that only time and attention can deliver. A quick glance at my trees, veggies, soils or flowers and I can tell if they're thirsty, hungry or happy. I've become part of a living ecosystem that needs my care to thrive. And through this connection, an understanding of timelessness can creep in. For our whole existence, humans have always interacted with Earth in some capacity. How we do that has been informed by the past (as we learn from one another) and will shape what comes next (as we pass on what we know). The type of gardening and farming we do now is a direct message to our future generations; this is sometimes called 'legacy gardening'. We can time travel through gardening by thinking about what type of mark we're going to leave on the earth – and making sure it's a good one.

And just as we impact the earth, we impact each other. I increasingly believe that building relationships with people (our community) and place (the land we live on) is perhaps some of the most important work we can do. Bridging social gaps brings us to a place of compassion and respect. And closing the ever-growing gap between us and natural ecosystems reminds us that we *are* Nature.

If we work towards building strong bonds with people and place we can help write a new story for how to be in the world. A story based on cultivating living connections of care. A story laced with multigenerational thinking and pointed towards intergenerational justice. A story that's grounded in a series of ever-evolving relationships that cross generations. And holding all that together is the bigger story that goes like this ...

Everything that is most true and dear is:
    grounded in plain love
    and the knowing that we all
    Share the same earthbeat.

Conclusion: For life

As a child I gardened
because I had to.
As a young adult
I gardened to help shape a
better world for all.
As an older adult I garden
to help shape a better
world and me for all.

For me, gardening transformed from being a boring job as a kid when I helped my dad in the herb nursery to a deeply significant life venture. Now every moment spent with my head, heart and hands engaged and grounded in gardening, farming and landscape care creates life-enhancing meaning for the world and helps me be me. Once I found my meaning, I was hooked. I could see the direct link between landscape health, human health and whole ecosystem health. I don't reckon it's an accident that the word 'human' has its roots in 'humus' meaning soil or earth.

> 'Nobody needs your garden. You're doing it for the meaningfulness you find in it.' – Alexander Okenyo.

We garden for many reasons. To be useful; to save money; to improve or maintain our physical, mental and spiritual health; to connect with people, place and culture; to express creativity; to heal, to protest, to restore fresh thinking and feeling, to process grief; and to contribute to the story of crafting a better future.

But as my online survey captured, most of us (over 94 per cent of us) garden simply because it brings us joy.

Ever since I was little I've wondered why humans garden when they don't have to, and so I'm left with wild delight that I've been able to answer that question with this book. These pages are the culmination of hundreds of interviews and decades of curiosity. In fact, I've unknowingly been working on this book in my head for over two decades. My dear husband has been the guinea pig for many half-formed ideas, but he has also been the source of great inspiration.

Once, after an impressively rambling chat that included climate doom and exploring our relationship to cockroaches, Anton voiced one of the most perfect sentences: 'Maybe that's what gardening is — it's just being on life's side, that's why we garden.'

We garden for life. You know when you hear something and you feel your gut responding? Well my gut said a big YES to this. Anton and I garden to be on life's side. We garden in order to be our full and free selves and to look after the living ecosystems we're part of. We're participating in life and perpetuating it, passing it to the next generation in the form of a thriving garden.

- 'It grounds and connects me to natural beauty, clears my mind and nourishes my soul.' **Christine F**
- 'I garden because I live.' **Sidonie Carpenter**
- 'Gardening is a form of magic I think in which you start to converse with the world more deeply. It is ancient and also very much in the moment and for the future. Truth to be spoken, the garden grows me.' **Pippa Buchanan**
- 'It is my happy place to see the miraculous abundance,

beauty and gifts of nature unfolding. The rewards of eating unadulterated food and the joy of sharing produce and experiences with fellow gardeners. Some mornings I even feel my plants welcoming me with reciprocating love.' **Anonymous**

- 'Nourishment of soul.' **Anonymous**
- 'I need to feel connected with the natural world, and growing things helps me feel "real" in the face of so much artificial and man-made landscapes.' **Linda M**
- 'I garden for what it gives me: visitors – native and human. Habitat not just for birds and animals but a beautiful peaceful place for us. Nourishment – vegies, herbs, all our senses, exercise, creative expression. Gardeners are great sharers, of ideas, cuttings, experience, produce and encouragement. Gardening makes us all better people and it's accessible to all.' **Jill Merrington**
- 'I love being able to make even a small difference in the place where I live, for example planting shrubs that will encourage local native birds and beneficial insects and reptiles.' **Anonymous**
- 'I garden because I have no say in it, it's some sort of primal desire that comes from within me.' **Julie V**
- 'I believe gardening is in our human nature. I want to contribute to creating/initiating diversity leading to abundance and resilience and a healthy ecosystem. It makes so much sense.' **Doris L**
- 'I can't explain it really, but it feels like a deep instinctual calling. All my life it's the one thing I keep coming back to for joy and connection with earth/spirituality.' **Shannon**

Gardening helps connect and ground us so that we can remember who we are. It encourages us to send down our taproots in place and time to deepen this sense of self and connect to the vital life force that is running through us all. We do this so that we might have a good life, but when we're at our best we also do it to help others have the same. An authentic act of love.

In her book *All About Love*, bell hooks writes extensively that true, good love has the potential to be transformative for all involved. But for this to happen love has to be a combination of care and commitment – both *words and action*. When love is in action, people can support one another's spiritual growth and they're more interested in what they can give, rather than take.

This sprung to mind when I was talking with my friend Shani Graham in Perth, Western Australia. She was telling me a story of how at one of their community garden gatherings her partner, Tim Darby, asked people to complete the sentence 'gardening is …' Among all the answers was one that stood out to her: 'Gardening is the big love.'

This made my heart swirl. While I'm deeply interested in what edible produce I can take from my garden, I'm more interested in what I can *give to* my garden. I'm only healthy when my garden is healthy and my garden is only healthy when I'm healthy. We're in a relationship where we both strive to make the other the best they can be. You could say that we're in love!

I think of the thousands of hours I've had my hands in the earth, working it while it works on me. The countless times I've lain down on the ground letting the earth hug me as I sink into it remembering I'm just another animal in Nature. The way my garden brings me unending delight and the unconditional love I pour into it (the only other thing I love like this is my daughter). And if we remember how all our bodies came from the earth and will eventually return to it (and that perhaps our spirits are laced throughout it as well) then loving my daughter is also loving my garden. It's all connected and it's all love.

And this is where I land … that even when we don't have to, and sometimes without realising it, we seek out gardening to enhance life in every possible way, inside and out. And we do it for the love of life and that we might continue it.

So, get out there! Grow that pumpkin, plant that native tree, prune those roses, build that compost pile and water those seedlings. If you can, why not go camping in your backyard, courtyard or balcony garden. Be best friends with your patch and tell it all your secrets – it'll plant them in the earth and keep them safe. While you're at it, make time to lie down on the earth and breathe it all in. Take off your shoes and let as much of your body commune with this garden planet as possible.

And at the end of the day, at the end of our lives, we'll all turn back into a garden of sorts. The late organic gardener Peter Cundall said, 'Remember, old gardeners never die, they just gradually turn into compost.' What a glorious thought! All those microbes working hard to cycle and transform my body's nutrients into deep dark compost. Making my blood and bones available for plants to absorb me through their roots and shoot up towards the sky. What a delight to think that my life will make more life.

Yes, I like that … I like knowing that even once I'm dead I'll still be gardening. Building soil – the common ground for future gardens, generations and all of life and love to grow from.

Acknowledgements

Endless thanks to the hundreds of survey participants and dear friends for generously sharing some of your garden gold with me. Heartfelt hugs to Kitana Mansell, Jen Calder, Tim Winton, Laura Tingle, Clare Bowditch, Bruce Pascoe, Jane Edmondson, Jude Bennett, Costa Georgiadis, Bob Brown, my dad – Justin Moloney, David Stephen, Mickey Robinson, Lou McLachlan, Jess Bell, Anton Vikstrom, Sally Ives, Brenna Quinlan and Charlie Mcgee for going a bit deeper with me.

Solid editing kudos to Coco and Ruby at Affirm Press who were also very generous in the cheerleading department (appreciated).

Gigantic amounts of gratitude to dear Anton my sweet pea husband for being so good and supportive and kind and interesting and interested … And thanks to Frida Maria our daughter who couldn't care less about this and keeps me humble.

And a universe-size shout out to Earth for being the best (and only) planet to garden on, you're so beautiful.

Notes and references

1   Davis, M, 'Can inequality be blamed on the Agricultural Revolution?', World Economic Forum, October 2018, https://www.weforum.org/stories/2018/10/how-the-agricultural-revolution-made-us-inequal

2   *National Geographic*, 'Fertile Crescent', https://education.nationalgeographic.org/resource/fertile-crescent/

3   Crawford, GW & Fussel, GE, 'The Americas', *Britannica*, 11 June 2025, https://www.britannica.com/topic/agriculture/The-Americas

4   UNESCO World Heritage Convention, 'Kuk Early Agricultural Site', 2008, https://whc.unesco.org/en/list/887/

5   Beale, B, 'Papua New Guineans among world's first farmers', ABC Science, June 2003, https://www.abc.net.au/science/articles/2003/06/20/883719.htm

6   Hara, M & Von Glahn, R, 'Agriculture and Its Environmental Impact', Cambridge University Press, February 2022, https://www.cambridge.org/core/books/abs/cambridge-economic-history-of-china/agriculture-and-its-environmental-impact/CE57528C50EB10E5C662259695648F07

7   Nogrady, Bianca, 'Indigenous Australian fire-stick farming began at least 11,000 years ago', *Nature*, 11 March 2024, https://www.nature.com/articles/d41586-024-00693-6

8   Henry, David, 'Nikolai Vavilov: The father of Genebanks', *Crop Trust*, 10 January 2024, https://www.croptrust.org/news-events/news/nikolai-vavilov-the-father-of-genebanks/

9   Krznaric, Roman, *The Good Ancestor*, Penguin Books Australia, 2020

10 Thuras, Dylan, 'Vavilov Research Institute of Plant Industry', *Atlas Obscura*, 15 April 2016, https://www.atlasobscura.com/places/vavilov-research-institute-of-plant-industry

11 Swan, Norman, *So You Want To Live Younger Longer*, Hachette Australia, 2022.

12 Carrington, Damian, 'World's top climate scientists expect global heating to blast past 1.5C target', *The Guardian*, 8 May 2024, https://www.theguardian.com/environment/article/2024/may/08/world-scientists-climate-failure-survey-global-temperature

13   Food and Agricultural Organisation of the United Nations, 'Regional technical platform for family farming', https://www.fao.org/platforms/family-farming/recursos/experiencias/projects-detail/the-urban-peri-urban-and-family-agriculture-program-in-cuba-and-municipal-self-sufficiency-in-food-supply/

14   Levenston, Michael, 'Cuban urban agriculture meets its 2024 production target', *City Farmer News*, 27 December 2024, https://cityfarmer.info/cuban-urban-agriculture-meets-its-2024-production-target/

15   While the reasons for it have changed over the decades, America still has a trade embargo with Cuba, making it the longest-running embargo, starting in 1959.

16   Sustainable Soils Alliance, 'Soils and public health', https://www.sustainablesoils.org/about-soils/soils-and-public-health-2/

17   Corser, Gabrielle, 'Getting down and dirty in the National Soil Archive', CSIRO, 11 September 2024, https://www.csiro.au/en/news/All/Articles/2024/September/soil-archive-research

18   Aksoy, Melek and Logie, Sinan, 'Instanbul Gardens', 2016, https://www.nomasmagazine.com/istanbul-gardens/

19   French Gardens, 'French garden design', https://www.french-gardens.com/design/frenchgardendesign.php

20   Sims, Josh, 'The strange appeal of garden lawns', BBC, 29 April 2022, https://www.bbc.com/future/article/20220426-should-people-get-rid-of-their-garden-lawns

21   Ignatieva, Maria et al., 'Lawn as a cultural and ecological phenomenon: A conceptual framework for transdisciplinary research', Urban Forestry & Urban Greening, vol. 14, no. 2, 2015

22   Planet Natural, 'Lawn history', 23 November 2024, https://www.planetnatural.com/organic-lawn-care-101/history/

23   Kilvert, Nick, 'How environmentally friendly is your lawn? Is it time to rip up grass in favour of a greener alternative?', *ABC News*, 4 August 2019, https://www.abc.net.au/news/science/2019-08-24/vegetable-gardens-for-green-grass-environment-lawn/11427458

24   Paredes, Valeria, 'The human cost of a perfect lawn', *Friends of The Earth*, 24 September 2021, https://foe.org/blog/human-cost-perfect-lawn/

25   Villazon, Luis, 'Is the straight line a human invention?', *BBC Science Focus*, https://www.sciencefocus.com/science/is-the-straight-line-a-human-invention

26   Shout out to Director Alana Valentine, Musical Director Amanda Hodder, Designer Edith Perrenot, Producer Marnie Karmelita, Project logistics team Sally Richardson and Caro Watson.

27   Suttie, Jill, 'How nature can make you kinder, happier, and more creative', *Greater Good Science Centre*, 2 March 2016, https://greatergood.berkeley.edu/article/item/how_nature_makes_you_kinder_happier_more_creative

28   Permaculture is a holistic design framework used to create sustainable human settlements and ecosystem health. Developed by Bill Mollison and David Holmgren in the 1970s in Lutruwita/Tasmania, it can be applied to environmental, economic and social contexts.

29   Swan, Norman, *So You Want To Live Younger Longer*, Hachette Australia, 2022

30   University of Texas, 'Study suggests nutrient decline in garden crops over past 50 years', 1 December 2004, https://www.sciencedaily.com/releases/2004/12/041203100522.htm

31   Kindall, HW & Pimentel, D, 'Constraints on the expansion of the Global Food Supply', *The Royal Swedish Academy of Sciences*, May 1994, https://web.archive.org/web/20181011060735/http://dieoff.org/page36.htm

32   Offenheiser, Ray, 'The green revolution: Norman Borlaug and the race to fight global hunger', *PBS*, 22 April 2025, https://www.pbs.org/wgbh/americanexperience/features/green-revolution-norman-borlaug-race-to-fight-global-hunger/

33   Ibid

34   Lovell, Rachel, 'How modern food can regain its nutrients', BBC, https://www.bbc.com/future/bespoke/follow-the-food/why-modern-food-lost-its-nutrients/

35   Ibid

36   Science Direct, 'Green revolution', https://www.sciencedirect.com/topics/earth-and-planetary-sciences/green-revolution

37   Burns, A, 'VIDEO: After the harvest: There are concerns about links between a common herbicide and Parkinson's disease', *ABC News*, 1 September 2024, https://www.abc.net.au/news/rural/programs/landline/2024-09-01/concerns-about-links-between-common-herbicide-parkinsons-disease/104296830

38   Burns, King and Davis, 'Scientists work to unravel silent pandemic affecting farmers', *ABC News*, 31 August 2024, https://www.abc.net.au/news/2024-08-31/parkinsons-disease-may-be-linked-to-farm-chemical-paraquat/104188978

39   Utah State University, 'Food waste: Post WWII Era: 1945-1960', http://exhibits.lib.usu.edu/exhibits/show/foodwaste/timeline/postwwii

40   World Health Organization, 'Traditional medicine has a long history of contributing to conventional medicine and continues to hold promise', 10 August 2023, https://www.who.int/news-room/feature-stories/detail/traditional-medic-ine-has-a-long-history-of-contributing-to-conventional-medicine-and-continues-to-hold-promise and WHO Global Traditional Medicine Centre, 'Catalysing ancient wisdom and modern science for the health and well-being of people and planet' https://www.who.int/initiatives/who-global-traditional-medicine-centre

41   De Caterina, R, Montinari, M, Minelli, S, *'The first 3500 years of aspirin history from its roots – A concise summary'*, National Library of Medicine, February 2019, https://pubmed.ncbi.nlm.nih.gov/30391545/

42   World Health Organisation, 'Traditional medicine has a long history of contributing to conventional medicine and continues to hold promise', 10 August 2023, https://www.who.int/news-room/feature-stories/detail/traditional-medicine-has-a-long-history-of-contributing-to-conventional-medicine-and-continues-to-hold-promise

43   Fun fact: The US Department of Agriculture declared dandelion as the most nutritious vegetable ever (after the herb parsley). Grubb, Adam, & Annie Raser-Rowland, *The Weed Forager's Handbook*, CSIRO Publishing, 2025

44   Staiger, Christiane, 'Comfrey: ancient and modern uses', *The Pharmaceutical Journal*, 22 December 2007, https://pharmaceutical-journal.com/article/news/comfrey-ancient-and-modern-uses

45   Ivers and Astell-Burt, 'Nature Rx: Nature prescribing in general practice', *Australian Journal of General Practice*, Volume 52, Issue 4, April 2023, https://www1.racgp.org.au/ajgp/2023/april/nature-prescribing-in-general-practice

46   Worldwide Opportunities on Organic Farms (WWOOF) is a worldwide movement to link visitors (WWOOFers) with organic farmers, promote a cultural and educational exchange, and build a global community conscious of ecological farming and sustainability practices' https://wwoof.net/

47   Brenna co-created children's book *Costa's Garden: Flowers* with Costa Georgiadis.

48   Australian Indigenous Health*Info*Net, 'Country, culture and spirituality', https://healthinfonet.ecu.edu.au/learn/health-topics/social-and-emotional-wellbeing/country-culture-spirituality/

49   Uncle Max Dulumunmun Harrison was an initiated Yuin Elder and passed on 11 December, 2021.

50   Wu, Tim, 'The tyranny of convenience', *The New York Times*, 16 February 2018, https://www.nytimes.com/2018/02/16/opinion/sunday/tyranny-convenience.html

51   Led by Father Peter Kennedy, St Mary's was an important hub for social justice and a safe space for many. While I wasn't religious myself, I had huge respect for Father Kennedy. He welcomed the homeless and the queer community, supported the local Aboriginal mob, had banners saying 'Free Timor Leste' out the front of the church for years and even buried my mum with enormous

kindness. I was disappointed that, after decades of invaluable community work, he was fired by the Pope himself in 2009 for being 'too radical'.

52 Just so you know, I did start camping in my backyard once I got home. The only teething issue was the 3am wakeup call from our rooster, Samantha. Earplugs became an essential ingredient to a good night's sleep.

53 Briggs, Helen, 'Seeds of hope: The gardens springing up in refugee camps', *BBC*, 21 May 2018, https://www.bbc.com/news/science-environment-44174865

54 Ibid

55 Test Book, 'Thoughts of Mahatma Gandhi on education – know Gandhi's educational philosophy, quotes & views on curriculum', https://testbook.com/articles/thoughts-of-mahatma-gandhi-on-education

56 Eat Well Tasmania, 'Healthy food access Tasmania', https://www.healthyfoodaccesstasmania.org.au/ and Picone, Adrienne, 'Talking Point: Make a choice to end poverty (The Mercury Newspaper)', *TasCoss*, 17 October 2022, https://tascoss.org.au/make-a-choice-to-end-poverty/

57 I lovingly stole this idea from the City of Darebin in Victoria.

58 Green Guerillas, 'Our history', https://www.greenguerillas.org/history

59 From Kenya, Wangari Maathai established the Green Belt movement, an environmental NGO focused on planting trees, environmental conservation and women's rights.

60 Dhall, Kiran, 'What Is Guerrilla Gardening? A concise guide', *Earthed*, 23 July 2024, https://www.earthed.co/blog/what-is-guerrilla-gardening-a-brief-history-of-reclaiming-our-green-spaces/

61 National Museums Liverpool, 'Geri Augusto – the importance of okra to enslaved people', 10 August 2018, https://www.youtube.com/watch?v=KlGylKHTI4Q

62 Britannica, 'Gerrard Winstanley English social reformer', https://www.britannica.com/biography/Gerrard-Winstanley and https://www.earthed.co/blog/what-is-guerrilla-gardening-a-brief-history-of-reclaiming-our-green-spaces/

63 La Via Campesina, 'About La Via Campesina', https://viacampesina.org/en/international-peasants-voice/

64 Ellis-Petersen, Hannah, 'Fighting giants: eco-activist Vandana Shiva on her battle against GM multinationals', 28 April 2023, https://www.theguardian.com/global-development/2023/apr/28/fighting-giants-eco-activist-vandana-shiva-on-her-battle-against-gm-multinationals

65 Navdanya, 'Conserving diversity and reclaiming commons', https://navdanyainternational.org

66 Incredible Edible Todmorden, 'We are Incredible Edible Todmorden', https://incredible-edible-todmorden.co.uk/

67 Incredible Edible Todmorden, 'What We Do', https://incredible-edible-todmorden.co.uk/what-we-do/

68 Discover the Tarkine, 'Tarkine Carbon', https://discoverthetarkine.com.au/tarkine-carbon/

69 Food and Agriculture Organisation of the United Nations, 'Carbon Sinks and Sequestration', https://unece.org/forests/carbon-sinks-and-sequestration

70 Bob Brown Foundation, 'Takayna logging threats', https://bobbrown.org.au/blockade-takayna/

71 Philosopher Jonathon Lear and authors Joanna Macy and Rebecca Solnit write thoroughly around this.

72 The Good Ancestor, 'Resources', https://www.romankrznaric.com/good-ancestor/resources

73 Japingka Aboriginal Art, 'Aboriginal Dreamtime stories', https://japingkaaboriginalart.com/aboriginal-dreamtime-stories/

74 Nicholls, Christine, '"Dreamtime" and "The Dreaming" – an introduction', *The Conversation*, 23 January 2014, https://theconversation.com/dreamtime-and-the-dreaming-an-introduction-20833

75 Ibid

76 Stanner, WEH, *The dreaming & other essays*, Black Inc, Melbourne, 2009

77   Nicholls, C, '"Dreamtime" and "The Dreaming" – an introduction', The Conversation, 2014, https://theconversation.com/dreamtime-and-the-dreaming-an-introduction-20833

78   Murtola, A. M., & Walsh, S (Eds.), 'Who's Futures?', *Economic and social research Aotearoa*, Tāmaki Makaurau Auckland, Aotearoa New Zealand, October 2020, https://researchspace.auckland.ac.nz/server/api/core/bitstreams/b1b55df5-ef1c-4961-802f-3e878b2e7cc0/content

79   Ibid

80   Future Library, 'Information', https://www.futurelibrary.no/#/information

81   Farm It Forward, 'What we do', https://www.farmitforward.com.au/

82   'Jude & the Beanstalk', *Gardening Australia*, ABC TV, 1 April 2022, https://www.abc.net.au/gardening/how-to/jude-&-the-beanstalk/13823396